ENDORSEMENTS

Ben Dixon has written an amazing book that breaks down the prophetic ministry in such a way that even a child can understand and learn to prophesy everywhere they go! Not only can a child get it, but this book also will help all of those who already are seasoned in the prophetic. I was deeply inspired and learned so much from reading this book and applying the truths and revelations in my daily life! I have found this to be a great tool that has enhanced my ability to hear God's voice with greater clarity! Ben is an incredible teacher, husband, father and friend. He brings out and thoroughly explains the differences between the Old Testament and New Testament prophetic ministries with depth and articulation that is so easily taught, but, more importantly, caught! I am so excited to see everyone equipped to give prophetic words as a lifestyle everywhere they go! It is your birthright as a child of God!

**–Todd White, President and Founder of
Lifestyle Christianity and Lifestyle Christianity University**

We live in a time referred to as the Information Age, but it really should be entitled the "Misinformation Age." With all the confused voices, fake news, and internet theories that abound, what we need now more than ever before is to know the mind of Christ and the heart of the Father. The most important skill of this hour is to enter into the wisdom of Heaven. Ben's new book, *Prophesy*, is a right-on-time theme that must be assimilated and fleshed out in this generation. Ben is an emerging prophetic voice who is biblical, relevant, and profound. His unique insight compounded with his strong teaching gift makes this book a great treasure. I highly recommend this book as a must-read to all who want to grow in this timeless gift.

**–Sean Smith, PointBlank International;
author of *I Am Your Sign* and *Prophetic Evangelism***

I have known Ben Dixon for at least a decade through our ministry partnership. Each time we have ministered together has resulted in profound prophetic moments. Ben is a great teacher as he expounds God's Word with assured confidence and authority. He is also a captivating preacher who articulates the truth with great anointing and power.

In addition, Ben is a wonderful author who writes with profound prophetic insight. His book, *Prophesy*, contains truth from the Word of God that will greatly encourage, exhort, and edify individual believers and churches at large. I have been blessed by the insight carefully exposited by Ben in this book and I recommend it as a textbook for the study and teaching of prophecy and prophetic ministry. I believe that God will stir and bless everyone who reads these pages!

–Dr. Leslie Keegel, President, Foursquare Gospel Church, Sri Lanka; Chairman, Global Foursquare Church

Ben Dixon has given his life to helping develop Jesus followers who are able to hear God's voice and be used by Him in powerful ways for the Kingdom. Ben has a solid track record of training people to be God's mouthpiece in an authentic manner. He is constantly discipling others to hear, obey, and speak from a place of humility and Holy Spirit empowerment. Ben has a strong prophetic ministry and easily could have used it to show off his gifting, but instead has worked hard to develop others. This book will be a great resource for all who desire to be a more effective spokesperson for God.

–Dave Veach, District Supervisor, Northwest Foursquare District of Churches

Ben's perspective of spirituals is highly practical—and not at all spooky or kooky. He believes, as I do, that we can all speak words prompted by God's Spirit, but we do not become automatons without brains. We do not need to change our accents or use centuries-old style of language to utter words of keen insight and revelation.

That brings me to another reason why I encourage you to read Ben's book: he doesn't write or act like a showman who wants to wow the crowd by doing impossible-seeming tricks. Instead of being a magician, Ben is a mentor. He will help you learn to hear God's voice, and to speak what you hear. Even if you are not a reader, you will want to read this!

–Daniel A. Brown, PhD, Church-Planter;
author of *Embracing Grace* and *The Journey*

Prophesy, by my friend Ben Dixon, is both inspirational and instructional. Ben draws upon years of personal experience prophesying the word of the Lord and training others to do so in a way that is powerful but also down to earth. This book is a thorough treatment on what prophecy is and how you can prophesy. I recommend it for the curious, the beginner, or even the seasoned prophetic voice. The power behind this book lies not only in Ben's immense study and knowledge, but also his life of integrity and powerful experiences of walking out what he teaches. Ben has taught for my ministry in church gatherings, camps, conferences, and Bible college classes. His ministry has always brought about much fruit in those who have heard him, and he has an accurate track record in prophetic ministry. I wholeheartedly endorse Ben's ministry and his new book, *Prophesy*.

–John Hammer, Lead Pastor, Sonrise Christian Center

The church of Jesus needs prophets. Most Christians have never been discipled in the use of spiritual gifts because they think they're for someone else. Some carry an unfortunate view that prophets can't be trusted and that the gift of prophecy is optional for church health.

Ben Dixon steps into this dynamic and offers us great aid. Ben desires all to embrace the reality that we can prophesy to one another for mutual upbuilding—that we too may walk out Spirit-empowered lives according to God's directives. I believe *Prophesy* is a book that will move us forward in these matters. *Prophesy* is the product of nearly twenty years of learning with a deep desire to help as many as possible walk in God's provision through the Holy Spirit.

–Chris Manginelli, Lead Pastor, Mill Creek Foursquare

According to the apostle Paul, the primary purpose of those who walk in a prophetic office is to *equip the saints for the work of* ministry (Ephesians 4:11-12). This ministry is undoubtedly related to teaching and training Christ's church to hear God's voice and to speak prophetically what they have heard by God's Spirit.

Ben Dixon understands this principle and practice and has given his life to helping God's people understand how to hear God's voice and to speak forth what they have heard with a combination of humility and boldness. This book defines, defends, and describes the privileged responsibility of being enabled to prophesy in the name of the Lord. I highly and wholeheartedly recommend it.

–Dale Evrist, Senior/Founding Pastor, New Song Nashville

PROPHESY

PROPHESY
RELEASING GOD'S VOICE

BENJAMIN DIXON

Ignite Global Media
Lynnwood, Washington

Website: www.igniteglobalministries.org
Email: info@igniteglobalministries.org

Empowered by

Cover design by Marina Smith and Kevin Lepp
Attribution to https://www.vecteezy.com for a portion of the microphone graphic

Publisher's Cataloging-in-Publication Data

Dixon, Benjamin
Prophesy. Releasing God's Voice,; by Benjamin Dixon.
185 Pages cm.
ISBN: 978-1-950742-00-4   Paperback
          978-1-950742-01-1   ebook
          978-1-950742-02-8   ebook
1. Religion. 2. Prophecy. 3. God's Voice. I. Title

2019906295

I dedicate this book to my wife, Brigit Dixon.

You are a loving wife, a faithful friend, a dynamic mother, and a true lover of God.

I am so grateful for how you have believed God with me for what we can't always see.

Thank you for praying, loving, serving, believing, and persevering for what God wants in our life.

I love you!

TABLE OF CONTENTS

INTRODUCTION

It's true. There are many good books out there on the prophetic gift and ministry. In fact, I regularly recommend a handful of them. So why did I write another book on this topic? Well, that has a lot to do with my story of encountering Jesus. Before I even knew what it meant to prophesy, it started happening to me. I recall thinking, "Am I weird?"—UNTIL I began reading stories in the Bible that sounded similar to what was happening with me. I never asked to be prophetic. I never read about the prophets in the Bible and thought, "I want to be one of those guys!" Nor did I want to have a label that would somehow make others think I was more spiritual than they. To be honest, the prophetic ministry has brought a good amount of rejection, pain, questions, and, sometimes, loneliness throughout my journey.

I have received prophetic words that have literally changed my life. Additionally, I have watched the power of one prophetic moment wash away years of discouragement and pain in a person's life when nothing else had worked. This ministry is a treasure that God has given us, but it requires proper understanding and stewardship in order to receive the fullest benefit that God intends. I am well aware of the damage that has been done in the name of the prophetic. However, I believe we must reclaim this ministry and retrain the body of Christ to carry this precious blessing with passion, integrity, and clarity.

I know that I still have a great deal to learn in this specific area, but I am certain that what I have learned has the potential to help those who truly desire to know and grow prophetically. I wrote this book for those who are called to prophesy. I wrote this book for those who are skeptical of the prophetic. I wrote this book for those who want to learn how to help prophetic people develop. I wrote this book because I think we NEED the prophetic, which is the reason that God gave it to us.

What would it look like if every church had a healthy prophetic ministry? As I travel from church to church, I think about this very question. Most places seek to have sound teaching, passionate worship, strong leadership, and a compelling vision. However, I have not seen many churches that are developing a healthy and fruitful prophetic ministry. My hope is that this book will help clarify what the prophetic ministry truly is and why we should desire this for ourselves, our churches, and the world around us.

It is with this hope that I pray the words of the apostle Paul over every person who ever picks up this book and reads it: "Pursue love, yet desire earnestly spiritual *gifts,* but especially that you may ***prophesy***" (1 Corinthians 14:1, bold emphasis added).

Benjamin Dixon
Ignite Global Ministries
www.IgniteGlobalMinistries.org

Chapter 1

My Prophetic Journey

Jesus said, "My sheep hear My voice, and I know them, and they follow Me" (Jn. 10:27). Not only do I believe what Jesus said, but hearing God's voice has been my experience since the day I became a Christian. When you read the words of Jesus it seems quite clear that this is what He desires for everyone. In my first book, *Hearing God*, my primary point is that everyone can hear the voice of God personally. In *this* book my primary point is that everyone can hear the voice of God *prophetically*. By this I mean that God wants to speak to us *for others* in a way that reveals the person and purposes of Jesus.

In this book you will encounter lots of Scripture, testimonies of God's power, encouraging thoughts, and clear principles. But let's be honest: you will be reading all of this through the lens of my own personal perspective. While there certainly is nothing wrong with that, I think it's vital that you know where I am coming from if you are to appreciate the subject matter as seen through my eyes. God's supernatural power—and the prophetic gift specifically—have played a massive role in opening my eyes to the reality of Jesus. My life has been transformed, my thinking has been challenged, my doubts have been squashed...and there is no going back for me.

I have been immersed officially and thoroughly into the reality of what I am about to share with you. With this in mind, allow me to begin by sharing a bit of my own prophetic journey, very abbreviated but still (hopefully) with honesty and vulnerability.

A Supernatural Encounter with God

It was 1999 and my life seemed like a total mess. I was nineteen years old and already drug addicted, sexually immoral, and full of anger. Sure, I went to church growing up but it wasn't real to me. I thought church people were fake, church services boring, and the story of Jesus more of a fairy tale than a historical event or powerful reality. I knew many of the biblical stories: Jesus changing water to wine, healing a blind man, walking on water, casting demons out of people, etc. Here's the deal though: those stories were *only* stories to me. I didn't see those kinds of things happening today, which made it easy to dismiss the Bible, church, and the reality of God altogether.

As you can tell, I wasn't looking for God, but what I didn't realize at the time was that God was relentlessly pursuing me (Lk. 19:10). For about three months I faced a series of circumstances that forced me to confront my unbelief and reconsider my thoughts about Jesus Christ. One day during that time, I was at the grocery store buying some gum and the lady at the cash register randomly started talking to me about Jesus. I remember thinking, "Why are you talking to me about Jesus? I just want to buy some gum!" On another day, a friend of mine who I used drugs with was at my house, and while we were talking he said, "Ben, you know you're not cut out for this kind of life. You're supposed to be doing something else!" His comment looped in my mind constantly for the next several months.

I found these and many other seemingly "random" moments mostly irritating until I began to realize that maybe they weren't so random after all. One night I was driving toward the freeway, only about half sober, and approached the curve onto the on ramp at about 85 mph. Desperately, I hit the brakes, but it was too late;

my car spun out of control and I headed straight toward a cement barrier. I remember thinking, "I am going to die!" I was serious; I thought I was going to die right then and there. All of a sudden, my car abruptly stopped about fifteen feet from the cement barrier; so abruptly, in fact, that my head smashed into the window and both wheels on the driver's side bent underneath the car at a forty-five degree angle. As I stepped out of the car, I was completely perplexed about how this had happened, but the initial thought that came to my mind was, "God must have spared my life!" While this event was totally unexplainable, I still spent the next several weeks trying vainly to make logical sense of it all.

Not long after this, I came home one night and headed straight to my room. Dropping on the floor, I fell into deep thought about my life. My heart was pondering and wrestling over the reality of God, and in that moment, I said out loud, "Jesus, if you are real, then I need you to show me, and I will give you my life." This was a simple prayer that was simply answered. Immediately, I started to feel the presence of God in such a literal way that it completely shook me, and all I could do was cry. In the midst of this I had a vision (even though I didn't know what a vision was) of the many moments where God had been present in my life and I had never acknowledged Him. That night I experienced the voice of God in multiple ways. I now knew that God was real and that I would never be the same. When I woke up the next day, I didn't want the drugs anymore. I didn't want the sexual sin anymore. My anger against everything began to turn into love for people, and all I wanted to do was talk about Jesus. This was nothing less than supernatural. However, this was only my introduction to the God of the supernatural, as I would soon learn.

A couple of my friends became Christians around the same time I did. We were all hungry for the things of God, so we started a weekly Bible study together. During prayer at the conclusion of one of our studies, just as someone started to pray, something that felt like electricity touched my body from head to toe for about thirty minutes. I'm glad I was sitting in a chair; otherwise, I am certain that I would have fallen straight to the floor. I couldn't move. I couldn't speak. I was so overwhelmed by the presence of God that I wanted to sit there all day. I would later come to understand this encounter with the presence of God as the Baptism with the Holy Spirit. My love for Jesus and His Word, and my desire to talk about Him with everyone went from strong to completely off the charts. My new-found zeal was truly uncontainable.

Eyes that See and Ears that Hear

After I left the Bible study that day, something strange started happening to me. It was like my spiritual eyes and ears were opened in a way that I neither expected nor fully understood. It all started with a handful of recurring dreams about people I knew, dreams so vivid and clear that when I woke up, I thought they had actually happened. Guess what? Over the next several weeks, some of what I saw in those dreams actually *did* happen.

One night I dreamt that I walked into a small room with double doors where I found a group of men sitting there ready to have a Bible study. I sat down in the circle and looked over to the man who seemed to be the leader of the study and gave him my attention. He said nothing to me and I said nothing to him, but I noticed everything about him from the color of his hair, to his glasses, to his smile. Then, I woke up. The dream was over. I remember thinking, "That was odd." A week or so later a friend invited me to a Bible study at a local church, and since I was free that night I decided to go with him. Inside the church building we walked upstairs and into a room with double doors where a group of men were sitting together. I sat down with them right next to my friend. As I glanced over at the leader, I nearly fell out of my chair. Seriously, though, the leader of the Bible study was the same man that I had seen in my dream a week earlier. I had never met this man and had never been to this particular church. He smiled at me, introduced himself, and then proceeded to lead the Bible study for the next few hours. I honestly can't remember what the study was about because the whole night I was struck by the fact that I had seen this happen in a dream and had no idea why.

At the end of the Bible study that night, the leader pulled me aside and invited me to minister with him in a local prison at the end of the month. I agreed to go. About three days before we went to the prison, I had another dream, in which I walked into a gymnasium-sized room that was white from floor to ceiling. The floors were white, the walls and ceilings were white, and even the tables and chairs were white. All of a sudden, another door opened and hundreds of men wearing reddish-orange jumpsuits entered the room and sat down at the tables. Standing at the front with a microphone, I shared my personal testimony and presented a simple gospel message about how Jesus came and gave His life for the forgiveness of our sins. When I finished preaching, I gave an altar call and dozens of men came forward to respond to Jesus for the first time. That's when I woke up. I decided to write down the dream because, at this point, I was almost expecting something to happen.

Three days later I met up with my new friend from the Bible study and a group of guys that regularly ministered in prisons. When we arrived at the prison, I learned that we would be facilitating four church services in three separate areas of a very large prison. Half way through the day, we had already facilitated two church services and were headed to our third location, where we would have our final services for the day. The guards escorted us to the inmate cafeteria, which was the only building large enough to host the number of men who were expected to show up. We walked into the building and all I could see was white. White floors. White walls. White tables and white chairs. As we started setting up our gear for the service, one of the leaders asked me if I would preach the message. "Sure," I replied. I don't know why I said yes. I had never preached a sermon or even written a message, for that matter, but without thinking, I agreed anyway. In the far corner the large doors opened up and for the next five minutes I greeted hundreds of men wearing reddish-orange jumpsuits. The dream I had received flooded back into my mind and I was truly overwhelmed. I had literally seen this moment before it happened; everything about it, from the place, to the people, and even the preaching. After beginning the service with worship, I stepped up to preach a simple twenty-minute message about the forgiveness that is found in Jesus. Just as in my dream, I gave an altar call and over thirty men came forward and huddled around me to pray that God would forgive them for their sins and give them new life through Christ. At that point in my life this was probably the most powerful moment of prayer that I had ever experienced.

Dreams like this instilled in me a deep hunger for the supernatural and an expectation that God would share things with me prophetically. I started praying regularly for people at my church and everywhere I went. As I prayed for people, I often saw prophetic pictures or heard simple phrases from the Holy Spirit. I shared so many of these prophetic moments with people that others began to expect prophetic ministry from me as well. I didn't always have words for people, and even when I did, they weren't necessarily detailed, life-altering prophecies about their future, but they always came with strength, encouragement, and comfort (1 Cor. 14:3). I knew this was real but didn't know how to explain it to people around me, even when what I said came true. I needed to learn more about what this was and what the Bible said about it.

I decided to talk to a pastor about what was happening, and it quickly became very clear to me that he thought I was either exaggerating or delusional. He basically told me to "stick to the Bible!" So, I did. I read the Bible every day. Some days I read the Bible for several hours. The more I read the Bible the more I realized that God speaks to people through dreams, visions, pictures, and many other ways. This encouraged me greatly. I read about Abraham, Jacob, Joseph, Gideon, Daniel...and the list goes on. All of these people received dreams, visions, and prophetic words from God, and that was enough to convince me that what I was experiencing was from God as well. But the fact was that I didn't know what I didn't know, and I needed to find a person or a place where I could learn and grow in my understanding and practice of the prophetic ministry.

Let the Training Begin

I had no idea where to start learning, so I decided to visit a bunch of different churches. I live about 35 minutes north of Seattle, Washington, so I searched around my area first and found only one church that talked openly and consistently about the gifts of the Spirit, or prophecy, in particular. I then broadened my search to a one-hour radius from where I lived. To be honest with you, I couldn't find much. That isn't to say there weren't any churches or ministries out there that could help me grow in the prophetic; I just couldn't seem to find them no matter how many churches I attended. I was pretty discouraged. I went to the local Christian bookstore to buy some books about the prophetic gift. While perusing the small Charismatic section, my eyes fell upon a book with a red and black cover. Written by a man named John Paul Jackson, its title was, *Unmasking the Jezebel Spirit*.[1] It sounded like an interesting book, so I began to read a little of it in the store. Information in the back of the book mentioned that the author was prophetic, so I bought it and in just two days read it from cover to cover.

Wanting to learn more about the author, I logged on to his website. To my surprise, I discovered that John Paul Jackson actually had a school that offered classes on hearing God's voice, prophetic ministry, and dream interpretation. These classes were located all over the country, but it so happened that at the time they had one starting at a church in eastern Washington, about five hours from my house. I signed up and within a few months was on my way. I drove out to eastern Washington several times in order to take all the classes, each of which were three days long and six to eight hours per day. I was immersed into a prophetic world that completely normalized what I had been experiencing for the previous two years. During our classes we studied almost all the visions and dreams in the Bible. We practiced prophetic ministry for hours by praying for one another, sharing what we heard, and allowing for feedback to determine if what we said was right or wrong. We even had opportunities to go out to local stores and businesses to pray for people and share the prophetic words that God put in our hearts. These classes were a launching pad for me and a great starting point for my prophetic journey.

During this time, I learned a great deal from many well-known prophetic ministers throughout the body of Christ. I bought tons of books and audio teachings that I went through dozens of times. These teachings helped to broaden my foundation as I grew in my understanding and practice of the prophetic gift. I also read about the historic revivals of Wales and Azusa Street, as well as the more recent modern revivals like the Jesus People Movement, the Toronto Blessing, and the Pensacola Outpouring. I quickly learned about the Prophetic and Charismatic conferences being held all over the United States and attended every one I possibly could. I was so hungry for the presence and power of Jesus. I had many incredible experiences going to all of these events, but I must admit that I also saw lots of weird, strange, bad, and even abusive examples of the prophetic ministry. When people share about the abuses of spiritual gifts, I know what they are talking about. While the bad is out there, it's important that we don't allow those examples to become a stumbling block to developing the real thing (1 Th. 5:19-22).

During this time, I attended a Prophetic Conference in eastern Washington. I showed up at the venue, registered, and headed to get some coffee. While I was standing in line, a man got in line behind me, so I turned around and began a conversation with him. It was mostly small talk. However, when I learned that he was the speaker for the conference that night, I suddenly felt the pressure to say something "important"; you know what I mean. He pulled me aside and, without even praying, began prophesying over me. "You are going to write books, you will prophesy, and go to many nations......." This prophecy went on for several minutes, and to this day I think I can only remember about half of it. As a 23-year-old, all I really heard in that moment was, "You are awesome, you will be awesome, and awesome is in your future." I mean, everyone wants to hear a prophecy of prominence, right? Of course, we never think about the work involved or the sacrifices that are necessary to fulfill such a prophecy. I sure didn't. All I know is that I felt awesome because someone told me that God was going to use my life in a way that would matter. This was the first of several prophetic affirmations that called me into an emphasis and cultivation of the prophetic ministry.

Some time passed, and now I was a youth pastor at a church in Kirkland, Washington. On one particular Sunday morning our lead pastor asked me to preach the sermon for our main service. As I finished the sermon and closed the service, a first-time guest walked right up to me and said, "God has called you to train people to hear the voice of God and to prophesy!" He shared a few more things and then asked if he could pray for me. "Please do!" I said. As he began praying, I was overwhelmed, and afterwards thanked him for sharing the prophetic word. Also, I gave him my phone number so we could stay in touch. A few weeks later the same man called and left a message on my phone. When I called him back, he said, "The Lord gave me a dream last night. You were teaching people about hearing God's voice, just as I told you a few weeks ago. Only this time, I heard the Lord say that you need to start giving away what you have or you will lose it." We talked for a little longer, and I thanked him for sharing this with me. To be honest, I wasn't really sure what to do with what he said.

At that time, I was struggling seriously with rejection, and while I didn't hate myself, I definitely wasn't the kind of person who thought God was going to use me in some significant way. I think this is why, in part, I had so many prophetic affirmations. I may have needed them to activate what the Lord wanted me to do. However, I really didn't know what the next step was. And while I questioned the "you will lose it" comment, I knew I needed to do something.

Freely You Have Received, Freely You Shall Give

In a window of about two years I transitioned churches, married my wife Brigit, became a stepfather to her two boys, and started a real estate career. I continued to receive prophetic confirmations and carry a burden to train people to hear God's voice, but I was still trying to find the best way to implement what was in my heart. I decided to take about five months off from work to develop some materials that would aid me in discipling people to prophesy. It was during that time that I wrote my first training manual, which was the seed of my book, *Hearing God*, and even this book that you are reading right now. I connected with some people at my church who were hungry for the presence of God and started a regular meeting in my home. Over thirty people showed up at our first gathering, but we managed to squeeze into my living room. I had a simple model that I still hold to this day: teach people from the Bible, demonstrate how to hear God and prophesy, and give space for everyone to do the same. We hosted our home group every month, but after our second gathering we simply didn't have the space to accommodate the amount of people who wanted to participate.

We moved the home group to our church and called the monthly gathering "Hearing God." By the second year we had over one hundred people gathering with us every month and it was still growing. While there certainly was a core of consistent people attending, we also had scores of new people from different age groups, areas, and churches. The people certainly came to learn, but most often they came to receive a personal prophetic word and see if God would use them to give one. We implemented several different hearing God exercises that were effective at training people how to minister prophetically. One common exercise we used was to have a few people stand in front while everyone else in the group prayed for them.

Then I would walk through the aisles, passing around the microphone to those who sensed they had a prophetic word for the person standing at the front. Watching people give a prophetic word for the first time never got old. The testimonies were incredible as the God of the Bible became real to people through personal prophecy.

After about five years of hosting monthly "Hearing God" meetings, I decided to put together seminars and conferences so we could accomplish more training in a shorter amount of time. By 2013, including all of our different gatherings, we had probably trained about four thousand people in hearing God's voice and in prophetic ministry. I was literally seeing the fulfillment of what God said I was going to do through the words I had received. Going back to my original prophetic word that I was given in eastern Washington, I knew I needed to take all of my materials and put them into book form so we could share a biblical and practical perspective on this very important topic. I spent the rest of 2013 writing my first book, *Hearing God*, and launched it in 2014. We have used this book in our church and many others to establish the reality of hearing God's voice. Now, with this book, *Prophesy*, I want to take the next step in bringing vision, health, and process to the personal and corporate ministry of the prophetic.

While the discipleship of believers and the evangelization of the world remain the primary purpose of the church, I believe that God has given us the prophetic gift as a tool to help us accomplish the mission. My prophetic journey has been unique, and I think it illustrates how God works in many of our lives both directly and indirectly for His own purposes. It is with this in mind that I share the following principles and perspectives that we would ultimately hear the voice of God personally, release the voice of God prophetically, and heed the voice of God entirely.

Chapter 2

What is Prophecy?

If you were to ask 10 different people the question, "What is prophecy?" I expect you would get 10 different answers. While someone might get it right, most would get it wrong due either to ignorance (no teaching) or to confusion (wrong teaching). Either way, let's face it: much controversy exists over the issue of prophecy.

In my early twenties I attended a local community college where I was invited to a weekly class focused on "Bible Prophecy." This class was not a part of the school, but met on the campus after school hours. I still remember the invitational fliers prepared for the class because I had never seen anything like them before. Picture in your mind a multi-page flier with dark clouds, lightning, the earth being split open, angels with trumpets, a huge hourglass with time running out, and Bible passages written on a scroll announcing, "The end is near!" I was mesmerized by the flier and thought to myself, "This class sounds awesome!" Not only did I attend the class for several weeks, but I was able to get other people to go with me. The first week, I discovered that the class was facilitated by a Seventh-Day Adventist Church right down the street from the college. At that time, however, I knew nothing about denominations or their various theological perspectives on the meaning of "prophecy." As the class went on, it became clear that this particular church thought of prophecy in very specific terms. They believed that prophecy was divine revelation that God gave the prophets in the Old Testament in order to foretell future events. They also believed that prophecy is not something that God still gives today, but that we are responsible to interpret the prophecies written in the Bible so that we can properly prepare ourselves for future judgment or glory.

I didn't attend the class very long because I did not agree with the majority of their teaching on prophecy; I shared this story to illustrate that we all enter into this conversation with predisposed thoughts. Our church background, personal experience, theological training, or lack thereof have a lot to do with how we think and believe about prophecy. If you have been part of a charismatic church, depending on the style, you may think prophecy is something that happens in the middle of a worship service when someone gets up and says something like this: "Yea, I say unto thee, I am watching and will deliver thee if thou wilt come unto me," etc. Or, perhaps you were never taught anything about prophecy and do not know what to think about it. Regardless of your background or current thought process, it is essential that we take the time to develop a solid biblical foundation for what prophecy actually is so we can understand and embrace it as God intends.

Defining Prophecy

As we engage this topic, we must first realize that prophecy is multi-faceted. A simple definition will always fall short in conveying the depth, importance, and current operation of something so vital that God has given to us. However, I have landed on a very simple definition that we need to unpack, but will serve as a helpful guide throughout our study. I define prophecy as "*a message inspired by God, communicated* **through a person.**"

I define prophecy as "a message inspired by God, communicated through a person."

through a person." This definition, I believe, captures the crux of what prophecy actually is. The specific components of a prophecy, such as the message content, who it is for, who gets to share it, and how the recipient receives it, are variables that can change and will need to be discussed in much greater detail.

In addition to our working definition, I think it is important to make a clear distinction between the terms *prophecy* and *prophesy*, because many people, for some reason, tend to misunderstand, misspell, and even wrongly use these two words. The word *prophecy* is a noun; the word *prophesy* is a verb. *Prophecy* is what something is; *prophesy* is what someone does. As I just mentioned, a prophecy is a message inspired by God, communicated through a person (what it is). To prophesy is the act of someone communicating a message that is inspired by God (what someone does). Although these words are very connected in purpose and function, they are not exactly the same. I hope this clears up any confusion so that we say the right things when we talk about the prophetic ministry. As you can tell from the title of this book, my passion is for us to understand prophecy for the expressed purpose that all God's people would prophesy!

The Old Testament Hebrew word for prophecy is *nebuah*,[2] which is only used four times and simply means "prediction" (2 Ch. 9:29; 2 Ch. 15:8; Neh. 6:12; Dan. 9:24). The primary reason we don't see this word often used in the Old Testament is because the biblical writers didn't define the experience of receiving a prophecy by using the term itself. Instead, they used terms like "... the *word* of the Lord came to me..." (Ezek. 33:1 emphasis added) in reference to receiving a prophecy from God. Additionally, the Old Testament Hebrew word for prophesy is *naba*,[3] which is used 59 times. It means, literally, "to bubble up, to pour forth words like those who speak under divine inspiration."[4] The word prophecy and the function of prophesying are mostly associated with prophets in the Old Testament writings; however, there are a few rare occurrences where those who were not prophets prophesied as well (for example, see Num. 11:27; 1 Sam. 10:13).

In the New Testament, the Greek word for prophecy is *prophêteia*,[5] which means "the speaking forth of the mind and counsel of God,"[6] or "declaring the purposes of God."[7] Additionally, the Greek word for prophesy in the New Testament is *prophêteuô*,[8] which means, "speaking forth divine counsel or foretelling future events."[9] As a result of our brief study of the various words, I assume you can agree that the simple definition I introduced for prophecy is fairly accurate. Once again, we are defining prophecy as *a message inspired by God, communicated through a person*. Now that we have a clear and biblically-affirmed definition, let's break down the elements a little bit more.

— A message

A prophecy is a message, but we must remember that not all messages are the same. Some messages are meant for one person while others are intended for thousands. Likewise, some messages are meant for one generation while others are meant for multiple generations. In essence, there are different kinds of prophetic messages.

— Inspired by God

A true prophecy is always a revelation from the Holy Spirit concerning the will of God.

— Communicated through a person

The source of the prophetic message is the Holy Spirit, but the giver of the word is always a person. We have the awesome privilege of hearing what God is saying and conveying those messages to others.

The Different Kinds of Prophecy

As I mentioned before, not all prophetic messages are the same. This means that there are different kinds of prophecy, and we must understand this if we are to embrace the prophetic ministry of today. In our previous study we noted that all prophetic words fall into two primary categories: foretelling and forthtelling. Let's define these words clearly:

- *Foretelling* speaks of what the future will hold before it happens
- *Forthtelling* speaks forth the present priorities of God

Foretelling is primarily about predicting future events regardless of their magnitude. Forthtelling primarily involves declaring the truth of God in a current context. While prophecy is both foretelling and forthtelling, it seems like the majority of people think of it mostly as the foretelling of future events. In my opinion, the reason for this is two-fold. First, when we read the Bible and see many of the recorded prophecies about the future, we automatically associate the whole of prophecy as falling within this category. The second reason is that we don't tend to consider the broadness of the prophetic ministry in both Old and New Testament times. In other words, the Bible contains the persons, stories, and prophecies that are timeless truth needed for every generation, sometimes referred to as Bible Prophecy. However, there were many prophets who prophesied during the timeframe in which the Bible was written, and while their messages were important for the people of their day, they weren't meant to be preserved as Scripture for all people in every generation. Knowing this will help us to embrace prophetic words today. That said; let's break down the two kinds of prophecy further to better understand the difference.

Foretelling is similar to a meteorologist forecasting the weather, relaying information about what the weather will do in days to come. We find most of these kinds of prophecies in the Old Testament, but

17

the New Testament contains a few as well. A large percentage of prophetic foretelling in the Bible relates to the coming of the Messiah (Jesus Christ) and surrounding events. Here are a few examples:

- Israel would be divided into two kingdoms (1 Ki. 11:29-33).
- Jerusalem and the temple would be destroyed (Mi. 3:11-12).
- The Messiah would be born of a virgin (Is. 7:14).
- The Messiah would be born in Bethlehem (Mi. 5:2).
- The Messiah would be betrayed for 30 pieces of silver (Ze. 11:12-13).
- The Messiah would be a descendant of King David (2 Sa. 7:12-16).

Some scholars say that the Bible contains hundreds of Messianic prophecies. Regardless of the exact number, we know that many of these prophecies have been fulfilled, while others have yet to be fulfilled. However, these are not the only prophecies recorded in Scripture that carry a foretelling nature. For example:

- Amos prophesied about the fall of Israel (Amos 5:27).
- Jeremiah prophesied that Judah would return from exile (Je. 29:10).
- Joel prophesied that the Holy Spirit would be poured out on all people (Joel 2:28-29).
- Agabus prophesied that there would be a great famine all over the world (Acts 11:28).
- Agabus also prophesied that the Jews would arrest Paul and hand him over (Acts 21:11).

As you can see, the majority of the foretelling prophecies *recorded* in the Bible carried great significance that superseded the context in which they were spoken. However, this does not mean that there weren't thousands of prophecies given from then until now that foretold some aspect of the future for a person, place, or situation that was localized to the immediate context. It is for this reason that I believe the function of prophecy is the same today as it was in the days of the Bible. However, I don't believe that the scope of the message is the same because the canon of Scripture is closed (more on this later).

I have both given and received prophecies of a foretelling nature. Several years ago, I was preaching at a friend's church and a young man walked up to me and asked if I would pray for him to hear the voice of God more clearly. I was encouraged by his request and gladly prayed for him. When I finished praying, he asked me if he could pray for me, and, of course, I said yes. Placing his hand on my shoulder, he started to pray a general prayer. But then he paused, and then said, "In three days God is going to give you a gift that will take care of all your current needs." I thanked him for the prayer and prophetic word without saying anything of its accuracy. During that time, I was attending Bible college online, assisting a church plant, and working 30 hours per week at a local company. I had just incurred a few unforeseen medical bills totaling 450 dollars and had no means to pay it. The day I received this prophetic word was a Thursday, and on Sunday I showed up at my home church and started setting things up for the service. Before long, a man walked up to me, handed me an envelope, and said, "Hey, Ben, I forgot to give this to you last week, but here you go. God bless you, man!" I walked outside and opened the envelope to find a check made out for more than enough to pay for all of my outstanding bills. The word I received had three specific details that all came to pass as they were spoken: the young man said that I would receive a gift (not income or expected); it would come in three days; and it would take care of all my current needs. This was a prophetic word that foretold a future event in my life, and it was powerful.

Forthtelling can be compared to the practice of free writing, where you basically write down whatever comes to your heart or mind without trying to figure out how it all flows together. The obvious difference between freewriting and prophetic forthtelling, however, is that with forthtelling the flow and words come from God's Spirit and not just our thoughts. This kind of prophecy may overlap with foretelling by carrying an aspect of the future, but it is primarily focused on God's mind, heart, and will for the current moment or situation. The Bible contains several examples of forth-telling by persons but without recording the message:

- Eldad and Medad prophesied among the Israelites (Numbers 11:26).
- Saul prophesied in the midst of the company of Prophets (1 Sam. 10:6, 1 Sam. 19:23-24).
- Peter spoke by the Spirit that what the believers were experiencing and the people were witnessing was the fulfillment of a prophecy from the book of Joel (Acts 2:14-21).
- The disciples at Ephesus were filled with the Holy Spirit and began to prophesy (Acts 19:6).
- Paul told the Corinthian church that prophecy would disclose the secrets of the heart and cause people to recognize the reality and presence of God (1 Co. 14:24-25).

This kind of prophecy is more common and can range in purpose from declaring the character of God to speaking wisdom into a person's current circumstance. Sometimes, a person can give a forth-telling prophecy that may appear to be simply good advice, wisdom, or just a "good word." However, what makes it prophetic is that it is a revelation from the Holy Spirit in that moment. It is my opinion that the majority of prophecy, perhaps 75 percent, falls within the forthtelling category.

Recently, I attended a house gathering to encourage a group of people who were in the process of planting a church. I was able to pray for about half of the group and later received a testimony from one woman that provides a good example of forthtelling prophecy. She writes:

Recently, Ben Dixon joined our gathering to encourage our church plant. I had been in a difficult and challenging season in many aspects, especially my health, that affected my eyes and autoimmune system. I was scared, had been searching for answers, and was feeling discouraged and alone. Ben prayed for me specifically without knowing anything going on in my life. He felt that God showed him Psalm 27:13, which happened to be a verse that the Holy Spirit had been stirring in my heart for the last several days. Ben then started talking about how God wanted to heal my eyes, open my eyes, give me vision; how He is changing my perspective and that I am carrying a lot of hope. This word was so right on to where I was at and what God was showing me. Truly it was a moment I felt so seen and loved on by God. From that point on, it was a catalyst for a big shift in my heart that helped me break through a wall I had in connecting with God through such a hard season. In addition, God has been consistently healing my eyes and revealing step by step how to walk in health.

When I prophesied over this woman, I did not have anything in my mind before I started praying. I simply did with her what I do in most situations like this; I began to pray and shared the thoughts that came to my mind. When I shared with her about God opening her eyes and giving her vision, I honestly wasn't thinking of it in physical terms, but, as you can see now, it was both. This is how forthtelling works, in many cases. You don't know what you are going to say in advance, but you learn to speak out prophetic words that bring edification, exhortation, and comfort (1 Co. 14:1-3).

The Source of Prophecy

Make no mistake: the Holy Spirit is the source of all true prophecy. There are other sources that cause people to say things that sound prophetic, but if their words do not originate in the Holy Spirit, they do not comprise real prophecy. In later chapters we will discuss false prophecy and the process for discerning true prophetic words, but for now we simply want to establish that the Holy Spirit is the sole giver of all true prophetic words.

Make no mistake: the Holy Spirit is the source of all true prophecy.

21

In Numbers 11 we find the Israelites, who have been traveling in the wilderness for some time, grumbling and complaining because of the difficulties they were facing. Their constant griping brings down severe judgment from the Lord. In the midst of this context, Moses appeals to the Lord that his leadership role among the people is a great burden that has become too heavy for him to carry alone. In response, God tells Moses to gather the seventy elders and bring them to the tent of meeting so that He can take from the Spirit that was upon him and cause Him to rest upon them all:

> *So Moses went out and told the people the words of the LORD. Also, he gathered seventy men of the elders of the people, and stationed them around the tent. Then the LORD came down in the cloud and spoke to him; and He took of the Spirit who was upon him and placed* Him *upon the seventy elders. And when the **Spirit rested upon them, they prophesied.** But they did not do* it *again* (Numbers 11:24-25, emphasis added).

As we can see from this passage, once the Spirit of God came upon the elders, they prophesied. We know that this is not an isolated occurrence because we continue to see this pattern throughout the Bible. The exact same thing happened right after Samuel anointed Saul as King over Israel (1 Sa. 10:10). Additionally, we read about Zacharias, the father of John the Baptist, who was filled with the Holy Spirit and prophesied just days after the birth of his son (Lk. 1:67). The prophet Joel prophesied of a day that would come in the future where the Holy Spirit would be poured out on all God's people, and as a result, THEY WOULD PROPHESY (Joel 2:28-29; Acts 2:17).

In the New Testament, the apostle Paul talks about prophecy as a spiritual gift. He makes it clear, however, that the Holy Spirit is the source for all spiritual gifts, including prophecy (Ro. 12:6; 1 Co. 12:4-11). A review of the various passages makes it abundantly clear that our theology of prophecy must be connected to our theology of the Holy Spirit. It is for this reason that we know there has been a massive shift in who can prophesy. Under the old covenant, the only people who prophesied were those who had been anointed by the Holy Spirit positionally as a prophet, priest or king. Under the new covenant in Christ, the Holy Spirit is poured out on all who call upon the name of the Lord; as a result, all can prophesy (Acts 2). Therefore, prophetic words are evidence to us that God's Spirit is moving in our midst, because He is the source of all true prophecy!

The Continuation of Prophecy

Many Christians today believe that modern prophecy is to study and interpret the Bible. In essence, this would mean that teaching and preaching God's word is equivalent to prophesying. This is simply not the case. This perspective does not come from the Bible but rather from a specific theological perspective called cessationism. A cessationist believes that all or most spiritual gifts are no longer given by God today. In support of this theology, cessationists often quote the following passage:

> *Love never fails; but if* there are gifts of *prophecy, they will be done away; if* there are *tongues, they will cease; if* there is *knowledge, it will be done away.* For we know in part and we prophesy in part; but when the perfect comes, the partial will be done away (1 Corinthians 13:8-10).

Cessationists interpret "but when the perfect comes" as the establishment of the canon of Scripture. In other words, once the Bible was canonized and available, there was no longer a need for the spiritual gifts, including prophecy. As a result of this thinking, many have changed the definition of prophecy to mean the interpretation of the Bible because, in their mind, God ONLY speaks in and through His word. Therefore, they view it as a violation of the Bible for anyone today to claim that God gave them a prophetic word. The above passage actually references Jesus at His return as "the perfect," which only further establishes the prophetic ministry for today. Don't get me wrong; I understand and respect the cessationists' desire to uphold the Bible as God's authoritative and eternal truth for all people in every generation—because it is. However, the definition of prophecy has not changed just because we now have the full Bible. The kind of prophecy that God gives to people today is not in competition with the Bible in any way whatsoever. The two simply don't have the same purpose. Look at what Peter said in his second letter to the churches that were scattered abroad:

> So *we have the prophetic word* made *more sure, to which you do well to pay attention as to a lamp shining in a dark place, until the day dawns and the morning star arises in your hearts. But know this first of all, that no prophecy of Scripture is* a matter *of one's own interpretation, for no prophecy was ever made by an act of human will, but men moved by the Holy Spirit spoke from God* (2 Pe. 1:19-21).

Peter, as a direct disciple of Jesus, was an eyewitness of His coming glory (Mt. 17:1-13) and the power of His resurrection (Mt. 28:16-20). He was able to affirm the fulfillment of prophecies recorded in the Old Testament as one who literally saw it happen before his eyes. In the above passage, Peter declares plainly that *no prophecy of scripture* was produced merely by men. The Holy Spirit moved upon the writers of Scripture, similar to the manner in which a wind carries a ship along the water. However, we need to acknowledge that there is a massive difference in scale between a personal prophetic word for someone today and a prophecy of Scripture.

When God spoke to the writers of Scripture, He made sure that there was 100% clarity in their receiving of revelation and 100% accuracy in their writing down of His revelation. For Scripture to be written as the eternal word (voice) of God, there could be no misunderstanding or wrong interpretations involved. This is not to suggest that God doesn't care about the clarity with which we hear Him today; I am here simply emphasizing the sovereignty of God over the process of Scripture coming to be. God did not allow the

Bible to be wrong; therefore, as a vehicle for hearing God, the Bible is in a unique category all its own.

When we seek to hear God's voice and prophesy today, we need to be clear that we are not seeking to contradict or rewrite the Bible. The written word of God is fixed and final. Its purpose is to provide all people with a clear standard concerning that which God wants us

When we seek to hear God's voice and prophesy today, we need to be clear that we are not seeking to contradict or rewrite the Bible.

to know. It does not and will not change throughout all generations. The Bible contains unchanging truths, such as the character of God, the fall of man, the plan of salvation through Jesus Christ, and Christ's second coming. The purpose of the Bible is to provide an unchanging foundation for all and to establish a standard by which *everything* we hear God say in the present is to be measured.

In later chapters we will explore the purpose and power of modern-day prophecy, but for now, I want to be clear in saying that God still speaks prophetically through people. While the prophetic messages that God gives today are not on the level of Scripture (which is fixed), they are still important, beneficial, and needed in our world today. Otherwise, God would not give them.

Chapter 3

Everyone Can Prophesy

Today, truly, we are living in one of the most significant and consequential times that our world has ever seen. While everything in the world seems to be getting darker and darker, the church of Jesus Christ is getting brighter and brighter. In the midst of these difficult times God is unifying His people and equipping us to be a compelling representation of Jesus to those around us. The world needs Jesus. We know this is true, but we must not forget that we are the means by which God reveals his Son to those who have yet to know him.

It is so crucial that we, as the church, know who we are, what we are called to do, and make ourselves familiar with the tools God has given us to fulfill His purposes in our generation. What we read about in the Bible is what God wants to do in and through us. Do you believe that? It always starts with what we believe! We pursue what we believe. We practice what we believe. That is why it is imperative for us to fully own our beliefs in order to see biblical realities established in and through our lives.

God has been restoring biblical truths and Holy Spirit-infused ministry to His church for hundreds of years. History shows this to be true regarding many topics, from the grace of God to spiritual gifts. The focus of this book is on one such ministry that God is restoring and releasing to the church in an unprecedented way. The prophetic ministry has a very important role among God's people, but I have found that many don't realize what is actually available to them. My intention with this book is not to bring you some new revelation, but, rather, help you understand what is yours in Christ.

The consequence of being a Spirit-filled church means that we are a prophetic people. We are not just the hands and feet of Jesus to our world, but also His prophetic voice that speaks life, love, hope, and divine destiny to those who need to hear it. And guess what? Everyone needs to hear it. Not only that, but I think people actually *want* to hear what God would say to them. If this is true, then

We are not just the hands and feet of Jesus to our world, but also His prophetic voice that speaks life, love, hope, and divine destiny to those who need to hear it.

who will share with people what God is saying? Better yet, *who is able to share* what God is saying? Do we believe it is only a chosen few? Do we think this ministry is reserved to those more qualified, more eloquent, or more spiritual than the rest?

Let me be really clear here: not only can EVERYONE hear the voice of God *personally* (Jn. 10:27) but EVERYONE can hear the voice of God *prophetically* as well. That's right: *everyone can prophesy*. This doesn't mean that everyone will be a prophet, or that everyone is prophetically gifted, but Scripture seems clear in its teaching that what was once reserved for the few has now been distributed to the many.

As I said earlier, our theology of prophecy is directly connected to our theology of the Holy Spirit, who is the giver of all true prophetic words. Therefore, I think it's important to spend the rest of this chapter laying a solid theological foundation for the proposition that "everyone can prophesy." I will build this prophetic foundation by laying out some fundamental truths regarding the Holy Spirit. Let me encourage you to pay special attention to the rest of this chapter because I will use a plenteous amount of Scripture to establish this truth, which will flow through the remainder of the book.

The Holy Spirit Living in You

When Jesus stepped into His public ministry, He chose 12 *ordinary men* as His disciples (Lk. 5:1-38). These men had the privilege of sharing life with the Son of God for a little over three years. They listened to Him teach. They observed His miracles up close and personal. They even shared meals together on a daily basis. They were eyewitnesses of the life and ministry of Jesus Christ, which is one of the major reasons we consider their biblical accounts authoritative for our lives. Jesus chose them not only as His followers; ultimately, He would call them as His apostles (Lk. 6:13) to continue His ministry upon His resurrection from the dead and ascension into heaven.

Shortly before His crucifixion, Jesus told His apostles that He was about to be betrayed and killed, but that it would serve a greater purpose that they still did not understand (Jn. 13:21-14:6). His comforting words to them in the middle of that conversation revealed a significant shift theologically from the old covenant to the new covenant:

> *I will ask the Father, and He will give you another Helper, that He may be with you forever;* that is the Spirit of truth, whom the world cannot receive, because it does not see Him or know Him, but you know Him because **He abides with you and will be in you** (John 14:16-17, emphasis added).

Just a few chapters later, Jesus goes as far as to say that it is better for Him to go (death, resurrection, ascension) so that the Holy Spirit can come (Jn. 16:7). At that moment, there was no way that the disciples could understand how anything could be better than having Jesus with them physically. But there was! Jesus promised that the

29

Holy Spirit would come to live IN those who believe in the gospel and choose to fully trust and follow Him.

The reality of the Holy Spirit living in us makes it easy to understand Jesus' statement that all His people would be able to hear His voice: "My sheep hear My voice, and I know them, and they follow Me" (Jn. 10:27). The people of God will hear the voice of God through the Spirit of God. Those who were under the old covenant did not have the indwelling presence of the Holy Spirit, which means that if you are in Christ, you have a profound position before God that not all of His people throughout history have shared.

On the day that Jesus rose again, His disciples were gathered together, hiding and seized with fear. In that moment, He showed up and presented Himself to them: "So Jesus said to them again, 'Peace *be* with you; as the Father has sent Me, I also send you.' And when He had said this, He breathed on them and said to them, 'Receive the Holy Spirit'" (Jn. 20:21-22). The natural question for us is, "Why did Jesus do this?" Why did He breathe on them and say "Receive the Holy Spirit?" We find the answer all the way back at the beginning of the Bible.

In Genesis 2 we read the account where God created the first person, whom we know as Adam: "Then the LORD God formed man of dust from the ground, and breathed into his nostrils the breath of life; and man became a living being" (Gen. 2:7). God breathed His Spirit into Adam, which caused him to become alive. Later in the same chapter God tells Adam that if he eats of the tree of the knowledge of good and evil, he will die (Gen. 2:17). Adam and Eve, his wife, end up eating from that tree anyway, which brings death upon them and the whole human race (Gen. 3:1-19). It wasn't just physical death that was introduced through the disobedience of Adam and Eve, but spiritual death as well. After this event, every person ever born has come into this world spiritually dead and in need of a reviving work that only God can do (Eph. 2:1).

This brings us back to John 20:21-22, where Jesus breathes on His disciples and says "Receive the Holy Spirit." This is a re-creation moment that reflects on the very creation account we just read in Genesis 2. God's Spirit (breath) brought life when we were created, and God's Spirit brings life when we are re-created in Christ. Jesus' disciples received the Holy Spirit within and were made alive to God in Christ. This is often referred to as a "born-again" experience (Jn. 3:3) in many, if not most, Christian circles. We need the Holy Spirit to make us alive because we are born into this world spiritually dead as a result of our sinful condition. Therefore, every person who becomes a Christian will receive the indwelling presence of the Holy Spirit because no one can be a Christian without the Spirit of God living in them. We must understand this truth, yet realize also that this is not the only thing that the Holy Spirit wants to do in our lives.

The Holy Spirit Coming upon You

After Jesus' death and resurrection, He appeared to His apostles many more times in order to prepare them to carry out His mission (Acts 1:1-4). Not only had the apostles received the indwelling presence of the Holy Spirit, but they also had clearest example of what they would be doing from the last three years of being with Jesus. However, Jesus essentially told them that they still needed something before they were to embark on their mission of bringing the good news to all people. Jesus told them, "You will receive power when the Holy Spirit has come *upon you*; and you shall be My witnesses both in Jerusalem, and in all Judea and Samaria, and even to the remotest part of the earth" (Acts 1:8).

Before the apostles could be sent out as witnesses of Jesus, they needed the power of Jesus. This reference to the Holy Spirit coming "upon you" is often called the "baptism," "infilling," or "empowerment" of the Holy Spirit, depending on your church tradition or theological

Before the apostles could be sent out as witnesses of Jesus, they needed the power of Jesus.

training. Regardless of what we call it, we know that this specific work of the Holy Spirit was essential for the apostles if they were to fulfill the mission of Jesus. The Holy Spirit living IN us and the Holy Spirit coming UPON us are separate experiences that have different purposes, and in this we learn that the work and ministry of the Holy Spirit is multi-faceted.

In obedience to Jesus, the apostles returned to Jerusalem to wait for this promised power encounter that was soon to take place. Acts 2 records its arrival:

When the day of Pentecost had come, they were all together in one place. And suddenly there came from heaven a noise like a violent rushing wind, and it filled the whole house where they were sitting. And there appeared to them tongues as of fire distributing themselves, and they rested on each one of them. And they were all filled with the Holy Spirit and began to speak with other tongues, as the Spirit was giving them utterance (Acts 2:1-4).

Try to picture this in your mind: Jerusalem was buzzing with people from all over the Roman Empire because it was the day of Pentecost, otherwise known as the Feast of Weeks. A crowd gathered and listened in awe-struck amazement as the band of Spirit-baptized believers spoke to them in their own languages. This was clearly a supernatural occurrence when you consider that over 13 languages were spoken. Some listeners were amazed, some confused, and some even mocked the believers and suggested that they were drunk. At that moment, Peter, inspired by the Spirit, quickly quelled that false impression and boldly proclaimed the truth of what was happening:

But Peter, taking his stand with the eleven, raised his voice and declared to them: "Men of Judea and all you who live in Jerusalem, let this be known to you and give heed to my words. For these men are not drunk, as you suppose, for it is only the third hour of the day; but this is what was spoken of through the prophet Joel: 'AND IT SHALL BE IN THE LAST DAYS,' God says, 'THAT I WILL POUR FORTH OF MY SPIRIT ON ALL MANKIND; AND YOUR SONS AND YOUR DAUGHTERS SHALL

*PROPHESY, AND YOUR YOUNG MEN SHALL **SEE VISIONS**, AND YOUR OLD MEN SHALL **DREAM DREAMS**; EVEN ON MY BONDSLAVES, BOTH MEN AND WOMEN, I WILL IN THOSE DAYS POUR FORTH OF MY SPIRIT And they shall **prophesy**. AND I WILL GRANT WONDERS IN THE SKY ABOVE AND SIGNS ON THE EARTH BELOW, BLOOD, AND FIRE, AND VAPOR OF SMOKE. THE SUN WILL BE TURNED INTO DARKNESS AND THE MOON INTO BLOOD, BEFORE THE GREAT AND GLORIOUS DAY OF THE LORD SHALL COME. AND IT SHALL BE THAT EVERYONE WHO CALLS ON THE NAME OF THE LORD WILL BE SAVED'"* (Acts 2:14-21, emphasis added).

The explanation that Peter gave here is actually a prophecy found in Joel 2:28-32. This prophecy was written at least 400 years (and potentially 800 years) prior to this moment. Now the apostles understood what Jesus had been telling them concerning the Holy Spirit being with them, in them, and upon them! I find it interesting that the *prophet* Joel *prophesied* about people *prophesying* and this was what the Holy Spirit directed Peter to say on the day that the church was born. This passage basically tells us that when the Holy Spirit comes "upon" people, they will be able to prophesy, which is something we see a handful of times throughout the book of Acts.

I have heard many sermons preached using Acts 2 in reference to the birth of the church, the baptism with the Holy Spirit, and the overall ministry of the Spirit. But I cannot recall a single one that ever discussed WHY the term "prophesy" is mentioned twice in Joel 2 and recalled as an explanation in Acts 2 for what the believers were experiencing. These significant words spoken on a very specific day have more meaning, I believe, than most people have ever considered. I want to highlight this as we weigh the concept that "everyone can prophesy," which I believe is what this passage of Scripture is actually saying.

The first part of the prophecy says, "AND IT SHALL BE IN THE LAST DAYS," God says, "THAT I WILL POUR FORTH

OF MY SPIRIT ON ALL MANKIND" (Acts 2:17). What is the significance of this? Well, the first thing to note is the timeframe referred to as the "last days." This language may seem coded to us, but many scholars agree that the term "last days" indicates a timeframe that was inaugurated on the Day of Pentecost when Peter said this. Also, it is commonly accepted that the "last days" timeframe continues until the second coming of Christ, which is otherwise referred to in Scripture as the "Day of the Lord." This would mean that even as I write this in 2019, we are still living in the "last days." Of course, this would also mean that the Holy Spirit is still being poured out, which is an important piece of our conversation, since the stated consequence of this ongoing outpouring is a release of the prophetic voice among us. Notice how the writer of Hebrews uses the same terminology in referencing a shift from how God use to speak to His people in contrast to how He does today:

> *God, after He spoke long ago to the fathers in the prophets in many portions and in many ways, in these **last days** has spoken to us in His Son, whom He appointed heir of all things, through whom also He made the world* (Hebrews 1:1-2, emphasis added).

The next thing we want to notice about the prophecy is that the Holy Spirit will be poured out on "all mankind." This term has several meanings depending on the context. We must remember that this was a first-century Jewish setting and the apostles didn't yet have any real paradigm for the Gentiles (non-Jewish people) being an integral part of God's plan. "All mankind" certainly refers not only to Jews but also to Gentiles. This reference, however, goes much further than that. The prophecy goes on to say that "all" would include young, old, men, and women, along with the underlying meaning of Jew and Gentile. To sum this up, we could say that God will pour out His Spirit on all genders, generations, and nations who call upon the name of the Lord.

This stands in stark contrast to what we see under the old covenant where the Holy Spirit did not indwell people and only empowered and spoke through those who were anointed to a specific office or calling before the Lord. The Old Testament mentions four specific callings that carried with them the empowerment of the Spirit and the ability to hear the voice of God and prophesy: prophet, priest, king, and judge. Obviously, these were places of leadership among God's people, which is why God anointed them with the Holy Spirit and spoke to them for the people. Therefore, the anointing of the Holy Spirit under the old covenant was positional, but now, under the new covenant, has become relational.

the anointing of the Holy Spirit under the old covenant was positional, but now, under the new covenant, has become relational.

Under the old covenant, a person who was anointed by the Spirit of God could lose that anointing if they deviated from their representation of God to the people. When King David was confronted with his sins of adultery and murder, he revealed that one of his greatest fears was to lose the presence of God through the Holy Spirit. He was the anointed king of Israel, and as a result experienced the Holy Spirit in a way that no common person could (1 Sa. 16:13). His sin not only misrepresented the Lord to the people but also brought about reproach against the nation of Israel from those who would hear about it far and wide. David knew that this sin might cause God to remove the anointing of the Spirit from His life, which was something that he did not want to happen, as we see from his lament in Psalm 51: "Create in me a clean heart, O God, And renew a steadfast spirit within me. Do not cast me away from Your presence And do not *take Your Holy Spirit from me*" (Ps. 51:10-11, emphasis added). As those who live under the new covenant, we never have to fear losing the Holy Spirit because our receiving and retaining the Spirit's presence in our lives is not based on position or performance as it once was.

Having the Holy Spirit come upon us in power is what enables us to prophesy. This experience was once reserved for certain people, but according to Acts 2 that is no longer the case. He once did not indwell people, but now He lives in those who place their faith in trust in Jesus. He once only empowered and spoke through a chosen few who carried specific positions, but now He will empower every believer and enable them to speak prophetically as a witness of Jesus. This is not to say that everyone is a prophet or that everyone has the spiritual gift of prophecy, but it does mean that through the Holy Spirit we can hear God for others and share with them what He is saying. The question is, has the Holy Spirit come upon you? Has he baptized you with power? Are you positioned to receive from Him in order to give away to others what He has given to you? Let me encourage you to seek God earnestly for the power of the Holy Spirit, and you can be sure that He will answer you because this is what He wants to do in your life!

The Holy Spirit Flowing through You

The Bible records several instances where someone prophesied right after the Holy Spirit empowered them (Nu. 11:25; 1 Sa. 10:10; Lk. 1:67; Acts 2:17), and we just established how this has become a new normal under the new covenant. As we are empowered by the Holy Spirit, we can prophesy, but just because something is available does not mean that it is operational. However, you can be certain that the Holy Spirit wants to flow through your life and release His prophetic voice.

Jesus talked about the release of God's Spirit through our life in this way:

Now on the last day, the great day of the feast, Jesus stood and cried out, saying, "If anyone is thirsty, let him come to Me and drink. He who believes in Me, as the Scripture said, 'From his innermost being will flow rivers of living water.'" But this He spoke of the Spirit, whom those who believed in

Him were to receive; for the Spirit was not yet given, *because Jesus was not yet glorified* (John 7:37-39).

In this passage, Jesus speaks of the Holy Spirit as a river, which is a powerful picture. A river is a natural flowing waterway that originates from a specific source and brings life everywhere that it goes. If the Holy Spirit is the river, then our lives are the riverbeds that channel the life-giving water to the people and places of our world. The Holy Spirit not only wants to live in us and come upon us; He also wants to flow through us like a mighty river.

I have seen people use a cup as a metaphor to illustrate how the Holy Spirit fills us up. However, when you think about this concept, it falls short in many ways. I think a better metaphor to use for what the Holy Spirit wants to do in our lives is a hose. He doesn't just want to fill us up; He wants to flow through us, which is exactly what Jesus said. Almost every day, I have the same prayer during my time with the Lord: "God, would you fill me with your Holy Spirit and flow through me so that people will somehow experience you in a powerful way?" God wants to release prophetic words through our life that become rivers of living water to refresh and replenish people all around us.

As you may recall my story from chapter one, several years ago I started a series of meetings which we called "Hearing God." People came from all over to learn how to hear the voice of God and prophesy. I really loved those meetings. Usually, I would ask this question before we broke up into groups: "How many of you have prophesied before?" When we first started, the number of hands raised were few, but as the months and years unfolded we saw those numbers significantly grow. During some of our first gatherings I had some friends in one of the groups who had never prophesied before. I basically told them to start praying for someone in their group and then share the passage, picture, or thought that came to their minds. As they began to pray for people in their group, God used them mightily to share clear and accurate prophetic words, which blew them away!

They had been Christians a long time but had never had an experience like that.

Not only does the Bible teach that everyone can prophesy, but this has been my experience with anyone willing to step out and share what they sense could be a word from the Lord. Prophecy is no longer reserved for prophets. Nor is it reserved for the gifted. Prophecy is something that can flow through any Spirit-filled believer who is willing to ask God and share with others. Are there still prophets today? Yes. Are there some who have a specific prophetic gift among us? Yes. However, these are not restrictions but rather specific designations of the gift. In his first letter to the Corinthians, the apostle Paul shares the powerful outcome of what will happen when all God's people begin to prophesy, and I pray that this would become our reality as well:

> But if **all prophesy**, and an unbeliever or an ungifted man enters, he is convicted by all, he is called to account by all; the secrets of his heart are disclosed; and so he will fall on his face and worship God, declaring that **God is certainly among you** (1 Corinthians 14:24-25, emphasis added).

Chapter 4

Prophets of Old

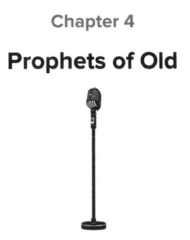

In order for us to move toward engaging the prophetic ministry in our world today, we first must understand the prophetic ministry of the past. While I certainly believe that everyone CAN prophesy, as we previously discussed, I want to make it extremely clear that not everyone is a prophet nor does everyone have a prophetic gift. However, I don't want to simply assume that everyone who reads this book will understand what a prophet is. Therefore, I want to take some time to look at the role and ministry of the prophet starting with the prophets of the Old Testament, whom I refer to as the "prophets of old" (Lk. 1:70).

The Scriptures reveal quite clearly that there were many prophets of Yahweh throughout the history of the Old Testament. The word "prophet" in the Old Testament primarily comes from the Hebrew word *nabi*,[10] which occurs more than 300 times from Genesis to Malachi. While this word certainly has a handful of definitions or variations, its most general definition is "an authorized spokesman."[11] This definition is quite broad, but many scholars seem to agree that it is hard to nail down a specific definition for this Hebrew word. However, the broadness of the word may prove helpful as we look at the differences between those who were called as prophets, especially when considering the diversity of their ministry.

Not all prophets in the Old Testament functioned the same way, carried the same authority, or even gave future predictions. For example, if you consider all the various words associated with and including the word "prophet," such as "seer," "watchman," and "man of God," you will come up with at least 40 specific references to different individuals. In addition to these references, we read about groupings of prophets like the "company of the prophets" (1 Sa. 19:20) or the "sons of the prophets" (2 Ki. 2:3), etc. Eight people in the Old Testament are identified as a "seer": Samuel, Zadok, Gad, Heman, Iddo, Hanani, Asaph, and Jeduthun. Of these, three (Samuel, Iddo, Gad) are also called prophets. There are two different Hebrew words that translate into English as "seer," but both basically mean "one who sees."[12] I have heard some teachers in the past say that seers were always prophets, but prophets were not always seers. There may be some truth to that, but it seems that seers were just prophets who primarily received revelation from God through visions or visionary type experiences (1 Sa. 9:9). Therefore, the term "seer" was more of a description of a prophet's function than a separate type of role altogether.

The White House Press Secretary performs one of the most important functions in the executive branch of the United States government. A senior US official, the White House Press Secretary oversees all the communications of the executive branch and acts as a spokesperson on behalf of the President across all media: print, broadcast, and Internet channels.[13] I imagine this is a very stressful job, because the person in this role does not have the luxury of communicating his or her own thoughts, views, or opinions, but has been entrusted to communicate on behalf of the highest office in the land and must do so in a way that is clear and accurate. The Press Secretary essentially is a messenger carrying the message of another.

This role has many similarities to the role of the Old Testament prophets, who had a special type of relationship with the Lord in that God spoke to them for the people. This great privilege carried a correspondingly great responsibility in that they were expected to speak the words that God gave them

Prophets were messengers with a message from God.

with complete accuracy. Prophets were messengers with a message from God. The book of Exodus contains a passage where God Himself gives a level of definition to the role of a prophet as he commissions Moses and Aaron to stand before Pharaoh:

> *Now it came about on the day when the LORD spoke to Moses in the land of Egypt, that the LORD spoke to Moses, saying, "I am the LORD; speak to Pharaoh king of Egypt all that I speak to you." But Moses said before the LORD, "Behold, I am unskilled in speech; how then will Pharaoh listen to me?" Then the LORD said to Moses, "See, I make you as God to Pharaoh, and your brother Aaron shall be your prophet" (Exodus 6:28-7:1).*

God called Moses to speak to Pharaoh concerning the Israelites, but Moses responded to God by telling Him that he was not skilled in speech and therefore unfit for the job. As a result of Moses' plea, God made a new arrangement involving Moses' brother Aaron. God would speak to Moses, Moses would speak to Aaron, and Aaron would speak to Pharaoh. In essence, Aaron became Moses' prophet. Think about this for a moment. In order for Aaron to be effective in his role, he would have to maintain a close relationship with Moses, pay special attention to what Moses told him, and courageously convey to Pharaoh whatever he was told. This is a clear picture of the function of a prophet as a messenger who conveys God's message.

As you follow the history of prophets throughout the Old Testament you will find that they say and do very different things from one another. Their calling, message, and audience may be different, but their source is always the same—God!

Prophets of Old Were Called by God

Search as you will, you won't find any person in the Old Testament who desired to be a prophet. It doesn't seem feasible that boys and girls grew up hoping that God would pick them for such a position. A prophet was called, commissioned, and anointed by God as His spokesman. There were many ways that God issued such a call, but a divine calling was necessary in order to affirm the messenger and establish their message with the proper authority. Carrying the role of a prophet could be quite dangerous (which may be one reason why nobody asked for it!). Many prophets were persecuted in the harshest of ways; some, even to the point of death (2 Ch. 36:16; Jer. 11:21; 18:18; 20:2, 7–10). In the book of Acts, a disciple named Stephen boldly questions the Sanhedrin by asking; "Which one of the prophets did your fathers not persecute?" (Acts 7:52). James mentions the prophets as an example of those who were patient in their suffering as they spoke in the name of the Lord (Ja. 5:10). My point is that nobody would sign up for this kind of rejection, ridicule, suffering, and possible martyrdom unless God called them to this position.

While Samuel was not the first prophet, he certainly was the beginning of a successive line of prophets that came after him (Acts 3:24). He started to hear the voice of God as a young boy (1 Sa. 3:1-14) and later was confirmed by all of Israel as a true prophet of the Lord (1 Sa. 3:19-21). In this we find that men confirmed the call that God had given. Samuel presided over a group of prophets that are referred to as the "company of prophets" or "schools of the prophets" (1 Sa. 19:20-21). Samuel carried a responsibility for the training and instruction of the future prophets of Israel. This does not mean that all prophets had to go through some kind of formal training that was instituted by Samuel, but it makes sense that with the acceptance of the prophetic role there was a clearer way to identify and establish credible prophetic voices. Being identified and affirmed by other prophets, as well as marked credible by the people, became part of the call of many prophets to come. Of course, this was not always the case. We have no idea where Elijah came from or how he was called by God as a prophet. Basically, Elijah just shows up on the scene and predicts a drought during the reign of King Ahab (1 Ki. 17:1). Additionally, Amos the prophet was not of a certain pedigree but was called from being a herdsman and a grower of trees (Amos 7:14). God had many ways of calling one to be His voice to people.

When Jeremiah was in his late teenage years, the Lord called him as a prophet to the nations (Je. 1:4-10). It's obvious from Jeremiah's response that this was something he neither wanted nor sought. Jeremiah suffered great persecution as a result of his prophetic call; according to tradition, he was stoned to death in Egypt because he rebuked the people for worshipping idols.

The prophet Isaiah, who was known for pronouncing God's judgment upon Israel and other nations, was called by God as a prophet through an incredible supernatural experience (Is. 6). Tradition tells us that Isaiah was martyred by being sawn in two[14] because he would not retract his prophecies of judgement concerning the evil deeds of King Manasseh (2 Ki. 21:16; He. 11:37).

God called prophets to be His mouthpiece. They were not necessarily leaders of the people, nor always received by the leaders of the people. Their prophetic role often caused them to be isolated from the politics and power that so easily corrupted those with the position and status to lead. They were called upon to carry the pure word of the Lord, which would range from affirming the decision

Prophets needed to know they were called by God if they were going to step into a ministry that had the potential of bringing about their own demise.

to go into battle, to pronouncing judgment upon a household or nation. Prophets needed to *know* they were called by God if they were going to step into a ministry that had the potential of bringing about their own demise.

Prophets of Old Heard from God

Old Testament prophets were mediators between God and His people, but they were not the only ones to have a mediator position. We know, in fact, that there were four different positions appointed by God to fulfill a mediator-type role: prophet, priest, king and judge. Prophets had a special role, whereby they received revelation from the Lord concerning people, situations, and nations. The Lord did not have direct relationship with the people where they could hear His voice personally, which is why he raised up prophets who represented Him in this way. As we will discuss in the next chapter, there is a massive shift in the role of a prophet from the Old Testament to the New Testament because of the shift that happens between God and His relationship to His people.

According to Scripture, God communicated to prophets in a few primary ways. There may have been other forms of communication that Scripture doesn't share with us, so we must stick to what we know. It was common for prophets to see visions, have dreams, or hear a direct word from the Lord, which most likely was audible.

Moses led the people of Israel through a forty-year journey in the wilderness in the hope that they might enter into the Promised Land one day. His siblings, Aaron and Miriam, assisted him in this journey the entire time. There came a point, however, where they were unhappy with their brother and began to question his leadership. This brought a clear and unequivocal response from the Lord:

> *Then the LORD came down in a pillar of cloud and stood at the doorway of the tent, and He called Aaron and Miriam. When they had both come forward, He said, "Hear now My words: If there is a **prophet among you**, I, the LORD, **shall make Myself known to him in a vision. I shall speak with him in a dream**. Not so, with My servant Moses, He is faithful in all My household; With him I speak mouth to mouth, Even*

openly, and not in dark sayings, And he beholds the form of the LORD. Why then were you not afraid To speak against My servant, against Moses?" (Numbers 12:5-8, emphasis added).

This story is quite startling for many reasons, but I am using this Scripture to highlight what the Lord said about prophets. He clearly makes a distinction regarding Moses as one who plays a more significant role than others, and at the same time sheds light on how He makes Himself known to prophets: through visions and dreams. Scripture shows us that many of the prophets, from Samuel to Isaiah, received visions and dreams. In addition to this, God communicated to several prophets through a direct word, such as we read about with Elijah: "Now it happened *after* many days that the word of the LORD came to Elijah in the third year, saying, 'Go, show yourself to Ahab, and I will send rain on the face of the earth'" (1 Ki. 18:1). Note in this verse that "the word of the Lord came to Elijah." This experience repeats itself with many others, such as Abraham, Samuel, Nathan, Isaiah, Jeremiah, Ezekiel, and more. It appears that receiving "a word from the Lord" was a direct word from God, either audibly or internally. Regardless of how it came, we know that it was exact wording so the prophet could articulate the prophecy with complete accuracy. Of all the things that a prophet was called to do, the first and most important was to hear accurately from God, because a prophet cannot be a messenger without a message.

Prophets of Old Established Covenant

Several covenants are mentioned throughout the Bible. A covenant is a binding agreement between two or more parties that often contain requirements or conditions. God established covenants through specific people, and I think it is worth noting that every person with whom God established a covenant was considered a prophet. This makes sense when you consider that the one receiving the covenant heard from God and carried that word in order to establish it for a future generation. This in and of itself is a prophetic act that echoes

45

into the future and impacts countless people and nations. God did not call many to carry this type of prophetic mantle, but those He did became a prototype of what was to come, and, ultimately, be fulfilled through Jesus Christ. In a sense, they were prophetic mediators of a covenant until the new covenant was established through Jesus.

Abraham is the first person the Bible refers to as a prophet (Ge. 20:7). In fact, God Himself is the one who references Abraham in this way. Most people wouldn't think of Abraham as a prophet in a classical sense because we never read about him prophesying like many others throughout the Old Testament. What we do see in the life of Abraham is a man who played a significant leadership role in God's plan through his faith and obedience to the voice of God.

God made a covenant with Abraham and promised him that through his faith and obedience He would multiply his descendants and give them the land of Canaan (Ge. 12:1-4; 17:1-22). Abraham received the promise of the Lord and walked in covenant with God, thereby carrying the prophetic word for and to the next generation. Scholars call this the Abrahamic Covenant. Consequently, Abraham became a Hebrew patriarch and a cornerstone to the promises and purposes of Israel and the nations of the earth (Ge. 12:3). This was a profound prophetic calling, and quite different from the majority of the rest of the prophets who appear in the Bible.

Moses was another man who established a covenant between God and His people and who was referenced as a prophet (Deut. 34:10). We learn from the book of Exodus that the Israelites were enslaved to the Egyptians for hundreds of years until God called someone to deliver them from their bondage. In fact, the Bible tells us that God heard the cries of the Israelites and remembered His covenant with Abraham: "So God heard their groaning; and God remembered His covenant with Abraham, Isaac, and Jacob. God saw the sons of Israel, and God took notice *of them*" (Ex. 2:24-25).

In Exodus 3, God encounters Moses supernaturally and calls him to confront Pharaoh with a simple message: "Let My people go" (c 5:1). Eventually, after at least 8 different confrontations, Pharaoh lets the Israelites go, and they head out into the wilderness with their final destination a place we often refer to as the "Promised Land." When the Israelites arrive in the wilderness, they come to Mount Sinai, where God had originally called Moses to deliver His people (Ex. 3:12). And it is on this mountain that God speaks to Moses about Israel becoming His covenant people:

> *Moses went up to God, and the LORD called to him from the mountain, saying, "Thus you shall say to the house of Jacob and tell the sons of Israel: 'You yourselves have seen what I did to the Egyptians, and how I bore you on eagles' wings, and brought you to Myself. Now then, if you will indeed obey My voice and keep My covenant, then you shall be My own possession among all the peoples, for all the earth is Mine; and you shall be to Me a kingdom of priests and a holy nation.' These are the words that you shall speak to the sons of Israel"* (Exodus 19:3-6).

When God says, "if you will indeed obey My voice and keep My covenant," He is referring to the Ten Commandments that He gives to Moses in the very next chapter (Ex. 20:1-17). Moses was first a prophet of God to Pharaoh; now he is a prophet of God to the Israelites. His prophetic call was to *mediate* a covenant relationship between Israel and Yahweh, which is often referred to as the Mosaic covenant. Moses spent the next 40 years relaying the conditions of this covenant to the nation of Israel before they finally moved into the Promised Land under the new leadership of Joshua.

Abraham and Moses each received a very unique prophetic call to establish covenants. This is not only unique from New Testament prophets, but from the rest of the Old Testament prophets as well. Only a few were chosen as prophetic prototypes before Jesus

Abraham and Moses each received a very unique prophetic call to establish covenants. This is not only unique from New Testament prophets, but from the rest of the Old Testament prophets as well.

came and established the new covenant. If we have no distinction among the prophets, then we will run into problems when we seek to explain the role of New Testament prophets, which were different in kind to Abraham or Moses. In the following chapter we will pick up this discussion as we look at how Jesus came to bring a new and better covenant, which brings about change to all callings and ministries, including that of a prophet.

Prophets of Old Wrote Scripture

One of the misunderstandings that I come across concerning the perspective of Old Testament prophets is that ALL of them wrote Scripture. This is simply not the case. The fact is that some Old Testament prophets wrote a book or two of the Bible, some wrote a passage of the Bible, some were mentioned in the Bible, and, of course, there were many whose words are not recorded in the Bible. Based on this we can conclude that while writing Scripture was not a primary call for most prophets, it certainly was for a chosen few.

Traditionally, the prophetic books of the Old Testament are divided into two groups that you will want to be familiar with: the "Major Prophets" and the "Minor Prophets." These designations are used to distinguish specific prophets and the scope or length of their message. For example, there are three Major Prophets: Isaiah, Jeremiah, and Ezekiel. Most scholars include Daniel and the book of Lamentations (ascribed to Jeremiah) among the Major Prophets as well. The "Minor Prophets" consist of 12 books named according to the prophet associated with each one: Hosea, Joel, Amos, Obadiah, Jonah, Micah, Nahum, Habakkuk, Zephaniah, Haggai, Zechariah, and Malachi. Again, the reason for the distinction has everything to do with the scope and size of each prophet's message. I am saying all of this simply to show that even among the prophets of old who wrote Scripture, there was quite a difference in the extent to which God used them in this way.

This function of writing Scripture is actually an important distinction between Old and New Testament prophets. No New Testament

Scriptures were written by prophets. The writers of the New Testament were either apostles, companions of the apostles, or unknown. You might say that the apostle John was a prophet because he wrote the book of Revelation, but I think it is best to consider him an apostle. This thought actually brings up an important point worth mentioning. Some theologians think that the apostles of Christ were the prophets of the New Testament, and that after them the office of prophet was no longer given. It may be that some of those who hold this view allow for prophetic gifts among the body of Christ, but they do not believe that any type of the prophetic office is for today. I think this view is wrong for a couple reasons. First, I think it implies that all prophets under the old covenant wrote Scripture, which they did not. Second, I think it implies that all prophetic words from God were and are somehow equal to biblical authority, which is not true.

Remember that the apostle Peter indicates a difference between a "prophecy of Scripture" from any other prophecy (1 Pe. 1:19-21). I am not saying that it didn't matter if non-Scriptural prophecies were accurate. However, it is reasonable to believe that non-Scriptural prophecies were more general than specific and carried more of a human interpretation than a dictation from God. If we hold that Scripture is God-breathed and authoritative for our lives, we are, in fact, saying that there is a difference between the revelation written in Scripture and the revelation that wasn't recorded. I believe that God sovereignly guided the revelation of Scripture, the reception of that revelation, and the transmission (writing) of that revelation. This is what sets Scripture apart from everything else and makes it entirely God-breathed (2 Ti. 3:16-17). As a result of this, non-Scriptural prophecy has a different purpose than Scripture and requires a process of discernment that we will discuss in greater detail in later chapters.

Prophets of Old Called God's People to Action

I commonly hear people refer to the prophets of old as those who were mad, sad, or angry, usually in reference to how they primarily spoke words of warning, correction, and judgement to God's people and the surrounding nations. Certainly, the prophets spoke difficult words, but this was only one aspect of their ministry. Additionally, long before bringing a pronouncement of judgment, they constantly exhorted God's people to make a righteous response to God. Over and over again, God used the prophets to call His people to action in multiple situations and for various reasons.

We must remember that some prophecies concern the absolute will of God that will come to pass regardless of human response. Other prophecies are an invitation from God to respond and thereby fulfill His will for our lives at the direction of His word. For this reason, when Old Testament prophets foretold the future, their prophecies often came with a rebuke and a call to repent. The difficulties Israel faced were mostly of their own making. The prophet's job was to name the sin and call the people to repentance before discipline or judgment became necessary. As you can see from this passage, the call to repentance and restoration was not a one-time thing but rather a constant offer from God through the prophets: "Yet He sent prophets to them to bring them back to the LORD; though they testified against them, they would not listen" (2 Ch. 24:19).

While Abraham and Moses were called to establish the covenants of God, the prophets who followed them regularly called God's people back to covenant faithfulness (Is. 58:1-12; Ho. 6:4-11; Mi. 6:6-8). All throughout the Old Testament the prophets exhorted God's people out of their complacency, falsehood, deception, idolatry, and disobedient actions.

Jeremiah's prophetic ministry revealed both the grief that God felt over Israel's disobedience as well as His desire to restore them for His glory:

All throughout the Old Testament the prophets exhorted God's people out of their complacency, falsehood, deception, idolatry, and disobedient actions.

"If you will return, O Israel,"
declares the LORD, "Then you

should return to Me. And if you will put away your detested things from My presence, And will not waver, And you will swear, 'As the LORD lives,' In truth, in justice and in righteousness; Then the nations will bless themselves in Him, And in Him they will glory" (Jeremiah 4:1-2).

Passages like these show us the heart of God for His people. God says through the prophet, "If you will return…" which is an invitation that would affect not only themselves but their children and generations to come. I often think that our misunderstanding of the Old Testament prophet is related to our misunderstanding of God throughout the Old Testament. If we think God is angry because He brought discipline and consequences, then of course we will think the prophets, who spoke words from God, were angry as well. The fact that we so often minimize the plea of the prophets for the good of the people and magnify the pronouncement of judgment reveals an issue that we have with God, and not just his messengers.

Prophets were not just robots who simply said what they were told to say. The Bible shares with us some intimate moments regarding the souls of the prophets as they revealed their own feelings and emotional responses to the words that they carried. They did more than share the word; they also felt and were affected by the words themselves. Jeremiah is often referred to as the "weeping prophet" because he was the one who pronounced the judgment upon Israel that resulted in the exile of their nation (Je. 9:1; 13:17). I can't even imagine what it would feel like to carry such a burden. God always has the best in mind for His people, but His people don't always yield to His best. The prophet lived with this reality every day. In this we learn something profound: the prophets were actually redemptive representatives to call God's people to action according to His will, and they often did so at their own expense. These representatives were a shadow of what was to come in the person and work of Jesus Christ.

Chapter 5

Prophets of Jesus

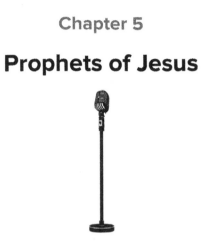

Several years ago, the lead pastor at my home church decided to preach a sermon series on spiritual gifts. It was a quite detailed study as he went through each spiritual gift mentioned in the Bible individually (Romans 12, 1 Corinthians 12-14, Ephesians 4). One of the ways he illustrated each gift was to identify a person in our congregation who exemplified the fruit of the gift he was highlighting that week. I thought this was a great way to teach through the gifts—until the day he talked about the prophets. I clearly remember the weekend that he focused on the calling of a prophet because he called me up on stage and talked a little about my life and why he felt as though this was the gift and calling the Lord had given me. I can't lie; it was awkward, not because of him but because I didn't refer to myself as a prophet, and neither had our church referred to anyone else as a prophet among us, at least publicly. After that day, the awkwardness I felt inside became an external reality with a handful of people who did not feel comfortable seeing me through this new lens. We learned very clearly that when you identify someone as a prophet, many reactions, assumptions, and presumptions arise based on past wounds, traditions, opinions, or personal theology.

This story brings up some important questions that we must address. Is there a difference between the prophets we read about in the Old Testament and those mentioned in the New Testament? Are there still prophets today? Is the gift of prophecy the same thing as the calling of a prophet? If everyone can prophesy, do we then really need to identify people as prophets? These are some of the questions that I hope to answer in this chapter. To be clear, I don't call myself a prophet, but I also do not try to stop people from thinking this way about me if they do. I believe that people can receive from the ministry that is on our lives regardless of what we call ourselves. Titles can be either helpful or hurtful, depending on the church culture we are part of or the people we are trying to reach.

Regardless of whether we use titles or not, identifying prophets for clarity's sake is important because there truly are prophets among us today and we need their ministry if we are to mature into the fullness of Christ (Eph. 4:7-16). We see the ministry of prophets throughout the New Testament, which is the foundation for why we believe their calling is still necessary today. Even the early church document known as *The Didache*[15] devotes half a chapter to the presence of prophets. In order to establish this conversation in Scripture, let me give you a quick snapshot of the New Testament references regarding prophets:

> **We see the ministry of prophets throughout the New Testament, which is the foundation for why we believe their calling is still necessary today.**

- Jesus told His disciples, "I am sending you prophets" (Mt. 23:34).
- Prophets are listed as one of the five callings that represent the fullness of Christ that will equip and disciple the church (Eph. 4:7-16).
- A group of prophets from Jerusalem were identified, along with a man named Agabus, as one of their primary voices (Acts 11:27-30, Acts 21:10-12).

- Prophets were identified in the city of Antioch (Acts 13:1-3).
- Two men named Judas and Silas are identified as prophets (Acts 15:32).
- Paul lists the calling of a prophet as foundational to the church (1 Co. 12:28).
- Paul gives instruction to the prophets in the city of Corinth (1 Co. 14:29).
- The church was warned about false prophets multiple times which indicates that there would be real prophets and we need to know the difference (Matthew 24:24, Acts 13:6, 1 John 4:1).

I can understand why some people have objections to the idea that there are prophets today, which is why we need to discuss it all the more. A considerable amount of erroneous teaching has occurred regarding prophecy, usually connected to the misuse and abuse that often surrounds it. Additionally, there *are* false prophets among God's people who try and elevate themselves over others in order to manipulate for financial gain or some kind of prominence. I get it. In fact, I have personally experienced some of these things myself.

Many years ago, I was introduced to a group of people who were connected to what was considered an apostolic movement. I attended several of their meetings and encountered a number of great things, including the demonstration of prophecy at an incredibly high level. At the same time, I was uncomfortable with their overuse of titles—among other things. I am not exaggerating by saying that pretty much everyone I met from this movement was considered either a prophet or an apostle. They liked titles—A LOT. They even called me a prophet within a month of knowing me. It wasn't long, however, before the bad started outweighing the good, which made me decide to move on. For myself, I wasn't offended by this group because I consider myself to be an "eat the meat and spit out the bones" type of person. However, I can certainly understand how others might be put off by the way these people stewarded the gifts of God.

This experience and many others have given me some understanding and compassion for those who struggle with someone being called a prophet in our world today. At the same time, the Bible tells us that God has called some to be prophets, even today, and we would miss what God intends if we choose not to embrace what He has given. That said, we cannot afford to develop our theology or the outworking of our ministry based on the wounds of the past or the bad examples we disdain. The obscure perspective of what a prophet is and does will only persist if we stay in ignorance concerning the presence and purpose of prophets among us. Throughout the rest of this book I will refer to New Testament prophets primarily as '"prophets of Jesus." My reasoning for this is simple: that is what they are.

Jesus is "The Prophet"

In our last chapter we discussed how the primary function of a select number of prophets was to establish covenant between God and His people. We read about how Abraham and Moses functioned as mediators of a covenant in both word and deed and that God used them to bring about His will in time and history. However, the story doesn't stop there. Something greater was coming and the prophets of old knew it. They didn't fully comprehend what lay ahead, but they were pointing to something—or should I say, someone—who would fulfill the longing they expressed (Mt. 13:17).

Moses spent His final days preparing the people of Israel to go into the Promised Land with loyal and obedient hearts. He was their leader. He was their mediator. He was their prophet. Sadly enough, Moses was not able to go with them on this journey because of his own disobedience to and misrepresentation of God among the people. Joshua was to take Moses' place of leadership as they entered into the land, but God told Moses that He was going to raise up a new type of prophet who eventually would replace him. This prophet would be like Moses, only greater:

I will raise up a prophet from among their countrymen like you, and I will put My words in his mouth, and he shall speak to them all that I command him. It shall come about that whoever will not listen to My words which he shall speak in My name, I Myself will require it of him (Deuteronomy 18:18-19).

The promise that God gave of raising up a future prophet was actually a Messianic prophecy about the coming of the Lord Jesus Christ. For some reason, some people have interpreted this passage of Scripture as identifying the calling of a prophet or further defining the qualifications of a prophet. I have even heard some Bible teachers use this passage to disqualify modern-day prophets if they don't meet the standards of 100% accuracy in their words from God. We must not interpret this passage any other way than as it was intended, which is to identify the coming Messiah, whom we know as Jesus Christ, and whom Scripture refers to as "The Prophet." Please don't misunderstand me. Jesus was certainly more than a prophet. However, as we consider the context of this passage, we note that this "Prophet" would come from Israel and reflect Moses' ministry. Jesus came as a Jew and He established a covenant—the New Covenant (He. 8:6).

Israel awaited the arrival of "The Prophet" and understood the difference between who this person would be and any other prophet among them. When John the Baptist was questioned about his identity, he was specifically asked if he was "the Prophet" (Jn. 1:21). The apostle Peter, while explaining the gospel to a crowd of Jews, referred to Jesus as "the Prophet" who was anticipated from the time of Moses (Acts 3:22). Immediately prior to his martyrdom, a disciple named Stephen defended the gospel before the Sanhedrin and clearly identified Jesus as "the Prophet" who was to come (Acts 7:37).

Jesus was not only "a" prophet but he was actually "THE PROPHET." He was like Moses in that he would have direct communication with God and would mediate a new covenant through His blood that would forever change the relationship between God and His people. The new covenant teaches us that Jesus is the only mediator we need: "For there is one God, and one mediator also between God and men, the man Christ Jesus, who gave Himself as a ransom for all, the testimony given at the proper time" (1 Ti. 2:5-6). It is through Him that all of us can be close to God and relate to Him as our heavenly Father.

John the Baptist made a very important statement that is often both misquoted and misunderstood. He said, "He must increase, but I must decrease" (Jn. 3:30). We cannot allow modern misinterpretation to cause us to miss the significance of this statement. John the Baptist was the last prophet of the old covenant. Jesus was the first prophet of a new and better covenant. John represented the old; Jesus represented the new. The "decrease" that John refers to regarding himself was not a personal comment regarding his stature or prominence but rather what he represented as a spokesperson for God. With the increase of Jesus, there was no longer a need for prophets as mediators between God and His people. That aspect of the prophet's role is clearly fulfilled and replaced in the person of Jesus Christ. Consider how the writer of Hebrews puts it:

In the past God spoke to our forefathers through the prophets at many times and in various ways, but in these last days he has spoken to us by his Son, whom he appointed heir of all things, and through whom he made the universe (Hebrews 1:1-2 NIV).

This verse does not mean that there are no longer any prophets today; neither does it mean that God no longer speaks to people. The writer of Hebrews is telling us that the role of the prophets to speak *for* God to the people is now completely fulfilled in the person of Jesus Christ, who is the final and greatest revelation of the Father. Now, every ministry, including that of a prophet, is **Now, every ministry, including that of a prophet, is subject to the mission, message, and ministry of Jesus, who shows us the way in all things.**

subject to the mission, message, and ministry of Jesus, who shows us the way in all things.

Prophets of Jesus: Similar, but Not the Same

The new covenant has surely ushered us into a new reality, where ordinary people can draw near to God, walk in relationship with Him, and hear His voice personally. Some take this to mean that the role of a prophet is no longer needed. That is simply not the case. The New Testament shows us that prophets still exist among God's people, but their role has changed in very specific ways. The old covenant prophet has been replaced by the new covenant prophet, and this transition brings with it a new job description for ministry. However, there are still some similarities between the prophets of old and the prophets of Jesus that are worth noting.

*What are the **similarities** between old and new prophets?*

1. Both hear the voice of God in various ways.
2. Both are called by God to be prophets.
3. Both are anointed by the Holy Spirit to prophesy.
4. Both have a uniquely marked life among God's people.

While I am sure there are many other similarities, these four seem to be the most distinct. Under the new covenant, prophets still have an important role, but it is one among a whole list of other important roles such as apostle, evangelist, pastor, and teacher (Eph. 4:11-13). Not only did the role of the prophet change, but so did other old covenant roles such as king, priest, and judge. The role of a king was replaced by Jesus who physically died on a cross with a sign above His head that read, "king of the Jews" (Lk. 23:38), and is revealed in His second coming as the "King of Kings" (Rev. 19:16). The role of priest has been transferred both to the people as a whole (1 Pe. 2:9) and to various gifted members of the body of Christ such as pastor and teacher (Eph. 4:11-13). Jesus, of course, is now and eternally our "great high priest" (Heb. 4:14). The role of the prophet has remained under the new covenant, but it is important for us to understand its differences from the prophets of old.

*What are the **differences** between old and new prophets?*

1. Prophets of Jesus do not write Scripture. While not all the prophets of old wrote Scripture, we know that some of them did and that it is no longer a function of prophets today.
2. Prophets of Jesus are not mediators. Now that all of God's people can hear His voice, the prophet's role has changed from being "the" voice of God, to being "a" voice from God.
3. Prophets of Jesus don't have exclusive authority. The prophets of old were not all accepted, but their role implied an authority that prophets today do not have. Prophets today are part of a team. Their words need to be discerned, because they know only in part and they prophesy only in part.

As with the similarities, I am sure that there are many more differences that I didn't mention. However, these differences are crucial because they are intertwined with the new covenant. If a person does not have a good grasp of the new covenant, it is likely that their ministry will be misguided at best and harmful at worst. Prophets in the new covenant are prophets of Jesus who manifest His words alongside His nature. This requires that we know the love of God in sending Jesus, the grace of God through the sacrifice of Jesus, and the ministry of the Spirit to draw all people to Jesus. We know what all of the prophets of old did not know (1 Pe. 1:10-12). We have what all of the prophets of old did not have. Therefore, our prophetic ministry must reflect what we know and what we have or it will not bring the results that Jesus gave His life for.

> **If a person does not have a good grasp of the new covenant, it is likely that their ministry will be misguided at best and harmful at worst.**

Prophets of Jesus Point to Jesus

The old covenant was based on the law. The prophets of old called Israel to obey the law, and when the people of God remained in their disobedience, the prophet, at times, pronounced God's judgement. They did this based on the terms of the old covenant between God and His people: if they obeyed, they would receive the blessings (Deut. 28:1-14), but if they disobeyed, they would receive judgment (Deut. 28:15-68). Here is the problem, though: nobody could ever fulfill the righteous requirements of the law (Ro. 3:19-20), which meant that judgment was inevitable. The law was righteous, and so were the correctional words of the prophets. However, the Scriptures teach us that no matter what the prophets said or how many times they said it, the people would not be able to fully obey (Ro. 6). Our world needed a savior. We needed a new covenant. This is why Jesus came into our world: "For the Law was given through Moses; grace and truth were realized through Jesus Christ" (Jn. 1:17).

Jesus came to offer grace. He lived without sin, voluntarily gave his life as a sacrifice for our sins, died on the cross, and supernaturally rose from the dead. Jesus is the grace of God. He did what we could never do, and He offers us forgiveness of sins and right standing with the Father if we place our trust in Him. Therefore, salvation is not based on how we behave but, rather, on what we believe. The new covenant is founded on this important truth, which obviously stands in direct contrast to the terms of the old covenant. We can receive grace from God because Jesus took our judgment. You may ask, "Why are you emphasizing this so much? I thought we were talking about prophets." Well, think about how these truths will affect the mindset and ministry of prophets as they receive and share words from God.

The new covenant affects everything. Prophets of old declared judgement when Israel did not adhere to the terms of the covenant or heed God's voice. Jesus came to earth and was judged for all sin, thus ushering us into a dispensation of grace where judgement is suspended until Jesus comes back, when He will righteously judge the living and the dead (1 Pe. 4:5). Prophets of Jesus must understand this if they are to properly minister in their gifting. I am not saying that God will never give words that are difficult, such as warnings or corrections (Re. 1-3). However, I don't believe that prophetic revelation is the primary way that God gives correction to people under the new covenant. In fact, I believe that Matthew 18 and other passages like it show that correction primarily comes through relationship (friends) and responsibility (leaders).

I have met too many people claiming to have the gift of prophecy or the calling of a prophet who do not understand the serious differences between the old and new covenant prophets. They speak in a way that implies exclusive, unquestionable divine authority. They marvel when people don't obey their words. They denounce churches, ministers, movements, and anyone else who doesn't agree with them. They focus heavily on warnings to the conclusion of judgement without realizing that they are manifesting elements of a prophetic ministry that is no longer for today. They take their prophetic cues from Isaiah, Jeremiah, Moses, or even Elijah as if they are the model for the New Testament prophet. While we certainly can learn and glean from the prophets of old, they cannot be our model for what a prophet is today.

Every member of the body of Christ is called to preach the gospel (Mk. 16:15) and make disciples of Jesus (Mt. 28:18-20). This is the message and ministry that have been passed on to all of us. The callings that some of us have, such as apostle, prophet, evangelist, pastor, or teacher, are interconnected to the mission that we have been given by Jesus himself. Therefore, prophets of Jesus must minister in such a manner as to point to Jesus. The religious leaders who opposed Jesus' ministry pointed to Moses as their prophet (Jn. 9:28-29). In the same way, prophets of Jesus are compelled to point to the person and message of the Lord Jesus Christ as the source and standard for all things.

Prophets of Jesus Strengthen People

Many years ago, I viewed a historic home that was built in the 1890s that became a point of learning for me. I walked into the basement and looked around for a while until I realized that the perimeter foundation of the home was much larger than I had ever seen. The house had three stories above the basement, which was quite large, but this foundation still didn't seem normal. I asked an inspector about this and he told me that it can be common for an older home to need its foundation strengthened. I learned that there are many reasons for a foundation to be strengthened, such as large cracks in the foundation, soil erosion, or a change in the water table underneath the home. In addition to these, building codes change over time, and as we anticipate future events, like an earthquake, we want to prepare the best we can, which may necessitate enlarging a foundation so that it is strong enough to withstand whatever comes along. The people that you hire to strengthen a foundation are skilled in assessing potential problems and implementing solutions that make your home stronger than it was before. I believe this can serve as a great metaphor for what prophets provide to the body of Christ and to people in general.

Prophets of Jesus strengthen people. They do this in many different ways, but the end result is that people are stronger in the Lord as a result of their ministry. Prophets have the ability to see the cracks in our foundations, hear the voice of God for solutions, and assist with the plans to make things stronger than they ever were before. We need the prophets of Jesus in the church and around our lives if we are to be at our best. To highlight this, here is a brief look at four different ways that the prophets of Jesus strengthen others.

> **Prophets of Jesus strengthen people. They do this in many different ways, but the end result is that people are stronger in the Lord as a result of their ministry.**

1. Prophets of Jesus prophesy

Have you ever received a prophetic word from someone that immediately released a new level of faith and confidence? I sure have. When you were young you probably heard the saying, "Sticks and stones may break my bones, but words will never hurt me!" The fact that we had to make up a saying to somehow build a false safeguard for our soul only shows how serious of a lie that was. The fact is, words have power. How much more, then, words from God? The apostle Paul describes the power of prophetic words in his first letter to the Corinthians: "But everyone who prophesies speaks to men for their *strengthening*, encouragement and comfort" (1 Co. 14:3 NIV, emphasis added).

Prophetic words "strengthen" us by releasing confidence, faith, clarity, and supernatural power that help us get up, step up, and speak up like never before. The prophet Agabus prophesied about a great famine that would take place, and upon hearing this, the believers responded by giving generously (Acts 11:27-30). Agabus also visited the apostle Paul and prophesied that he would be imprisoned. Paul responded with great courage in the face of adversity (Acts 21:10-14). Two prophets named Judas and Silas went down to Antioch and prophesied, which caused the believers there to be "strengthened" in the Lord (Acts 15:32). When prophets prophesy, we see God's strength released in us, which provokes an obedient response from us!

2. Prophets of Jesus equip

When the apostle Paul wrote to the church at Ephesus, he shared a unique perspective of how Jesus gave a measure of his gifts (apostle, prophet, evangelist, pastor, and teacher) to different individuals for the purpose of building up the church:

> But to each one of us grace was given according to the measure of Christ's gift. Therefore it says, "WHEN HE ASCENDED ON HIGH, HE LED

CAPTIVE A HOST OF CAPTIVES, AND HE GAVE GIFTS TO MEN." (Now this expression, *"He ascended," what does it mean except that He also had descended into the lower parts of the earth? He who descended is Himself also He who ascended far above all the heavens, so that He might fill all things.) And He gave some as apostles, and some as* **prophets**, *and some as evangelists, and some as pastors and teachers, for the* **equipping of the saints for the work of service**, *to the* **building up of the body of Christ**; *until we all attain to the unity of the faith, and of the knowledge of the Son of God, to a mature man, to the measure of the stature which belongs to the fullness of Christ* (Ephesians 4:7-13, emphasis added).

The word here for "equipping" means to prepare, make ready, or fully furnish. Prophets equip the church in the area of ministry for which they are specifically called and gifted. Therefore, prophets of Jesus teach and train the body of Christ to hear, discern, and share what the Holy Spirit is saying. When the church is equipped to hear the voice of God themselves and give prophetic words to one another, it brings great strength throughout the body of Christ.

3. Prophets of Jesus impart

Sometimes in Pentecostal-Charismatic churches you hear the term, "impartation." A church may have an "impartation" service, which basically means that certain leaders are going to pray for people to receive something from the Holy Spirit. I am well aware of this practice being abused or cheapened, which is both alarming and sad. Despite the abuses, however, we see moments in the Bible where people pray for others to receive anointing or gifting from the Holy Spirit, and it truly happens. I have personally experienced this in and through my own life as well.

In the book of Acts, we learn that when Paul and Barnabas were at Antioch, a group of prophets were present among them. As they fasted and prayed, the Holy Spirit spoke through one of the prophets and said, "Set apart for Me Barnabas and Saul for the work to which I have called them" (Acts 13:2). After this prophetic word, the prophets laid hands on them and sent them on their first missionary journey, which turned the world upside down. In order for Paul and Barnabas to embark on such a mission, they needed strength, which the Holy Spirit imparted through the prophets and their words. Additionally, we learn that the apostle Paul and the body of elders were able to impart a spiritual gift to young Timothy through a prophetic word and the laying on of hands (1 Ti. 4:14; 2 Ti. 1:6). When prophets are present and ministering in a healthy way, they function as catalysts of spiritual impartation, bringing courage and strength to all those around them.

4. Prophets of Jesus discern

Prophets carry a unique discernment that enables people around them to see more clearly. A prophet's perspective tends to provoke the question that we so often fail to ask in the midst of circumstances: "What is the Lord saying right now?" Discernment helps us know what God is saying in the midst of many voices and opinions. In the early church, the prophets would discern the source of teaching, prophetic words, and direction for the body of Christ (1 Co. 14:29-33). This function is still available today, and while prophets are not the only ones to offer this contribution, they certainly are wired to do so.

A prophet's perspective tends to provoke the question that we so often fail to ask in the midst of circumstances: "What is the Lord saying right now?"

Something I have heard time and time again is how helpful the perspective of a prophet has been. It can often be the opposite if a prophet does not have a healthy mindset, lifestyle or humble way about them as they share the discernment that God has given them.

The truth still remains that when prophets are functioning in a healthy way we are all stronger because of it.

How Do You Know if You Are a Prophet of Jesus?

We have discussed the theology, purpose, and function of prophets, but the question you might be asking is, "How do I know if I am a prophet?" Or maybe you are asking, "How do I identify someone else as a true prophet?" To help answer these questions, I have developed a short list that will aid you in discerning the calling of a prophet in you or around you.

1. The calling of a prophet

Have you received the calling of a prophet?

Before you can identify a prophet, you must understand the difference between the calling of a prophet and the gift of prophecy. What I have described throughout this chapter is the calling of a prophet. As we have discussed, one of the functions of a prophet is the gift of prophecy. However, there are people who are not called as prophets that still have the gift of prophecy (Ro. 12:6; 1 Co. 12:10). The concept that you can have the function of prophecy without the calling of a prophet is actually a New Testament paradigm. I have met plenty of people who are very prophetic but, beyond giving prophetic words, don't exemplify the characteristics of a prophet.

According to the Bible, everyone can prophesy, and all of us should desire to do so as Spirit-filled people (1 Co. 14:1-3). But does that mean that everyone can be a prophet? The simple answer is NO. Jesus gives the calling of prophet to whom He chooses and there is no evidence that this is something we can or should desire (Eph. 4:7-13). In order to identify someone as a prophet, we would want to know how they were called to this ministry. It could be that God spoke directly to them, or they received a prophetic word from someone else, but there is always evidence of a prophetic call upon their life.

2. The anointing to prophesy

Do you prophesy on a consistent basis?

We know that prophets prophesy. However, one thing that distinguishes prophets from others is the scope and consistency of their words. Prophets often carry a unique authority to give corporate, regional, and national prophetic words, depending on the level of their authority. Additionally, prophets don't usually have to ask God for prophetic words because they just flow to and through them based on their calling. Consistent prophetic ministry is evidence that the Holy Spirit has anointed someone who carries the calling of a prophet.

Prophets must have a history of giving accurate prophetic words that bear fruit. It is not enough for someone to tell you that God spoke to them prophetically about things that already exist. This can be a form of manipulation. The questions that I ask in determining if someone is a prophet or not are the following; Do they consistently prophesy? Do they give clear prophetic words? Are the prophetic words accurate? Do their prophetic words bear fruit? Is their ministry clear or confusing?

3. The confirmation of community

Has your prophetic call been confirmed by the body of Christ?

The calling of a prophet is given for the building up of the church. Therefore, this calling should be established and confirmed in the context of the church. I have encountered many who claim to have the calling of a prophet without any confirmation from the people around them. It is possible that the people who are connected to a prophet don't have the ability to embrace such a calling, but usually that is not the case. Israel confirmed that Samuel was a prophet (1 Sa. 3:20), and the church in the New Testament embraced and recognized prophets such as Agabus, Judas, and Silas, among many others. If a person claims to be a prophet but has no history of being recognized or confirmed by leaders, their church, or their personal community, I would be quite skeptical of that claim. Sooner or later, every prophetic call will require community confirmation in order to be the beneficial presence that God intends.

4. The passion for discipleship

Do you desire to equip others to prophesy?

One of the biggest differences between a person who is called as a prophet and one who has the gift of prophecy is the desire and corresponding fruitfulness in equipping other people. Prophets carry a burden to disciple the body of Christ into hearing God's voice, discernment, prophesying, and supernatural ministry. This burden may not be evidenced in a young prophet, but at some point it will become a passion as they develop in their ministry (Eph. 4:7-13).

5. The burden for holiness

Do you carry a burden for people to obey Jesus?

While I am sure that every leader desires for all people to live a holy life, it seems that the prophet carries a unique burden for the people of God to follow Jesus with full abandon. The prophets of old displayed this burden quite often as God used them to call His people to repentance and full obedience. Prophets of Jesus carry a similar burden as they provoke the people of God to walk with God personally and obey Him completely. As prophets mature and develop, they grow in sharing the truth in love while leaving behind the stigma of an angry personality, which is often associated with their ministry.

Chapter 6

False Prophets

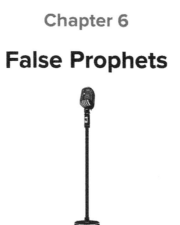

One morning I received an email from a man named Dave stating that he really needed to talk to me. He stressed that it was "very important." The message seemed genuine but I didn't have any time to meet in the near future, so I asked if he could share his urgent message through an email. Dave agreed, and a few days later he sent me a concerning message that I have never forgotten. "Hello Ben," his email began, "thank you for reading my message. A few weeks ago, somebody gave me your book, *Hearing God,* and as I began to read it I knew I had to talk with you." At this point, I assumed that Dave was about to tell me how much he loved the book and how it had blessed him (I had received those kinds of encouraging messages in the past). That is not what happened. "As I read the first couple of chapters," Dave continued, "I became very disturbed by your stories and by the way you referenced the Bible." At this point, I knew where Dave was going with this conversation, but I was still curious, so I asked him, "What are your concerns, Dave?" He replied; "Ben, you are misleading people with your book, and I believe that it's important for me to bring you correction. The Bible says that *false prophets* mislead people through doctrines of demons, lying visions, and counterfeit supernatural claims, which is what you are doing." Dave sent another handful of messages containing Bible verses and appeals to me to repent of my alleged sins. Through it all, he declared many times that I was not a Christian, but a false prophet who would give an account to God for how I was misleading people.

This was not the first time someone targeted me in this way; nor would it be the last. Now, let me assure you, I am not a false prophet and I am not sharing this to vindicate myself. The pertinent question is, why did Dave think I was a false prophet? He has never met me, has never been to my church, has never heard me teach or prophesy, and has no relationship with anyone who knows me. I am telling you this story because it illustrates an extreme version of a very common problem in the body of Christ today: we don't know what a false prophet actually is. I have heard the term "false prophet" thrown around many times in various circles, and it is my belief that our discernment on this very serious label has become clouded at best. In Dave's case, he thought I was a false prophet primarily because we have theological differences. Disagreement on theological distinctives does not give anyone permission to label someone else as a false teacher or prophet—but it happens all the time.

With that said, we should be aware that false prophets actually do exist and will continue to emerge until Jesus returns. In fact, Jesus plainly told His disciples that "many" false prophets would arise in order to mislead people (Mt. 24:11). The warning that Jesus gave concerning false prophets should provoke our sense of need for equipping and discernment to help all who are in our sphere of influence avoid deception and

I have seen way too many churches and individuals give up on the prophetic ministry altogether because the risk of something immature or false was greater than the potential of something authentic and fruitful.

falsehood. However, we must not allow our fear of the false to derail our desire and pursuit of the real thing. I have seen way too many churches and individuals give up on the prophetic ministry altogether because the risk of something immature or false was greater than the potential of something authentic and fruitful. Jesus did not warn us about the false in order that we give up on the authentic, but to make us fully aware that something as good and necessary as the prophetic ministry will be counterfeited by the enemy. As we develop a healthy prophetic ministry, we must be prepared to deal with false prophets and prophecy, which, unfortunately, tends to show up more often as we faithfully pursue the real thing.

What is a False Prophet?

The first thing we must recognize in this conversation is that we have an enemy. In his letters to the Ephesian and Corinthian churches, the apostle Paul made it clear that our enemy has *schemes* in order to deceive and destroy our lives (2 Co. 2:11; Eph. 6:11). We are at war with Satan and his demonic forces, who are constantly scheming our demise because they hate us and want nothing good for us. While our enemy has several weapons in his arsenal to use against the people and purposes of God, we know that chief among them is the weapon of deception. We see Satan wielding this weapon in the very beginning, when he directly questions what God has told Adam and Eve in order to get them to believe a lie (Ge. 3:4).

In the Bible, Satan directly attacks Adam and Eve, Jesus, and a handful of others. However, this is not how the enemy will attack us. Satan is not omnipresent; he cannot be in more than one place at one time. This means that our battle is primarily with demonic spirits who use all sorts of trickery to drive us off course. Demonic spirits will seek to deceive some individuals in such a way that they will actually become a voice of the enemy. In essence, that is what a false prophet truly is, a voice of the enemy. Paul said that "our battle is not against flesh and blood" (Eph. 6:12), but that doesn't mean that our battles won't involve actual people who have allowed themselves to be a voice from a demonic source.

To be clear: *a false prophet is a person who shares prophetic words or revelation from another source, either their carnal mind or a demonic spirit.* The intention of a false prophet is to lead people away from following the true God in exchange for a false one, whether the false prophet or an actual demonic entity. (Deut. 13:1-5). False prophets often will prophesy the exact opposite of what God has truly said (Je. 14:13-16), and will lie by telling people what they want to hear in order to gain a following for themselves (Ezek. 13). The fundamental issue regarding false prophets is that they are *not Christians*, and therefore do not have the Holy Spirit living inside them.

To be clear: a false prophet is a person who shares prophetic words or revelation from another source, either their carnal mind or a demonic spirit.

I have found that there are two kinds of false prophets that we must be aware of. First, there are those who literally represent and speak for another god. Throughout the history of the Old Testament we see many gods who were worshipped among the ancient Egyptians, Canaanites, and other people groups. All of these so-called gods had prophets who would speak for them, just as Yahweh had his prophets as well (1 Ki. 18:19). One of the reasons that the prophets of Yahweh would say, "Thus says the LORD," is because they were distinguishing which God they were speaking for. Whenever the word "LORD" is capitalized in the Old Testament, it is a substitution for Yahweh, the personal covenant name of God. Although the people of Israel were warned against consulting with those who practiced divination (Deut. 18:10) and listening to false prophets (Deut. 13:1-5), they still committed this sin repeatedly.

Modern examples of these kinds of false prophets would be leaders of other religions such as Islam, Buddhism, and Hinduism, or even cults like Mormonism and Jehovah's Witnesses. Mormons believe that their founder, Joseph Smith, was given a divine mission as a prophet of God to restore the true church and bring forth the book of Mormon. Muslims believe that their holy book, the *Quran*, is a divine revelation given to the prophet Muhammed by the archangel Gabriel. These men were false prophets who not only prophesied false revelation but also led people astray to follow another god, as we can clearly see today.

The second kind of false prophet is those who deceitfully present themselves as a true follower of God when they are not, and who share prophetic words, claiming God as the source when He is not. It is even possible that this kind of prophet actually believes that he or she is a true follower of God, but, in reality, is a wolf in sheep's clothing (Mt. 7:15-17). This is what Jesus was referring to when he said, "Many false prophets will arise and will mislead many" (Mt. 24:11). Not everyone in this category will call themselves a prophet, but they will claim that God/Jesus is the source of their revelation. There are many warnings in Scripture regarding false prophets and false teachers that call for discernment on our part when they are functioning among us (2 Pe. 2:1-2; 1 Jn. 4:1-3).

Distinguishing the Immature from the False

The majority of teaching regarding false prophets categorizes those with a prophetic ministry as either false or true. This is an extremely unhelpful view because it disallows any discipleship process for those who really are called as prophets, but who need help in developing their character and gifting. We currently have a whole system set up for the discipleship of pastors and teachers through our Bible colleges and seminaries. What is available for prophets? Well, I tell you this much—not much! If we are ever going to have a healthy prophetic ministry in the church, we will first have to embrace the fact that true prophets start out as immature, both in character and in gifting. It is not a sin to be immature, and it doesn't make you false if you are not 100% perfect as you grow in your ministry.

A few years ago, I met up with a group of youth and young adult pastors from different churches. We talked about all kinds of issues for a while and then the topic of spiritual gifts came up. Most of them knew that I had spent a large percentage of my ministry helping people to both understand and function in the gifts of the Spirit. As our discussion deepened, I could tell that one of the youth pastors had a significantly different view from mine regarding the function of spiritual gifts. He made a comment about the gift of prophecy that basically went something like this: "If you truly have the gift of prophecy, you never get it wrong. If it's from God, then it will be 100% accurate; otherwise, it's not from God." After he made this comment, many of the other pastors agreed without thinking through the implications of what he had said. I spoke up with a question. "Do you hold every gift and ministry to this same standard?" When he did not respond, I continued. "Are you telling me that every person who has a gift from God starts their ministry at 100% Jesus' level from day one?" This conversation went on for another hour or so as we debated the issue of discipleship in the area of spiritual gifts. What I was trying to show him was that he had adopted a view that allows some gifts to grow through discipleship and experience while others are either false or true. The end result of this kind of thinking is very clear: you won't have any prophets or prophetic gifts functioning among you.

Remember, false prophets aren't Christians. Immature prophets are Christians who are still in need of discipleship as it pertains to following Jesus *and* their gifting. True prophets WILL make mistakes, display character flaws, misinterpret and misapply prophetic revelation at times, and fail to adhere to wisdom principles in both life and ministry. Guess what—they

True prophets WILL make mistakes, display character flaws, misinterpret and misapply prophetic revelation at times, and fail to adhere to wisdom principles in both life and ministry.

are not perfect. This is actually true for all Christians and every calling that God gives to us for the same exact reason: we are all growing. While none of us has a license to willfully sin and disregard our failures as though they don't matter, we do have a license to grow—and there *is* a difference.

Sometimes I run across people who say things like, "The Old Testament says that any prophet who gives a prophecy that doesn't come to pass is to be killed!" My question is, "Is that what the Bible really says? This kind of comment comes from a reference found in Deuteronomy 18:

> **I will raise up a prophet from among their countrymen like you,** *and I will put My words in his mouth, and he shall speak to them all that I command him. It shall come about that whoever will not listen to My words which he shall speak in My name, I Myself will require it of him. But the prophet who speaks a word presumptuously in My name which I have not commanded him to speak, or which he speaks in the name of other gods, that prophet shall die. You may say in your heart, "How will we know the word which the LORD has not spoken?" When a prophet speaks in the name of the LORD, if the thing does not come about or come true, that is the thing which the LORD has not spoken. The prophet has spoken it presumptuously; you shall not be afraid of him."* (Deuteronomy 18:18-22, emphasis added).

You may remember from chapter 5 where I discussed this passage, noting that it is a Messianic prophecy. God told Moses that He would raise up a prophet like him. This is a specific reference to the coming of Jesus, who would establish a new covenant. We know that this was the interpretation Israel had for this passage of Scripture because it is interpreted this way later in the book of Acts (3:22; 7:37). To suggest that this passage is a good reference for how to deal with true prophets who misinterpret prophetic revelation or give a prophecy that doesn't come to pass is out of context and unhelpful. Truthfully, most people who have this view don't believe that there are prophets today anyway, so there is no use contextualizing the passage in that instance. I have never met a person with a prophetic calling or gifting who wanted to get a prophecy wrong or was somehow okay with it. Don't misunderstand me. I know there are plenty of misguided prophetic people out there, but I would consider them immature in their character and gifting rather than entirely false. Additionally, if immature prophets are not willing to be accountable, they don't deserve influence among us. But they shouldn't be regarded as non-Christians, as is the case with false prophets.

The accuracy of a prophetic word is not necessarily the primary way we determine if a prophet is false, because true prophets in their immaturity get it wrong sometimes. They may miss it by wrongly emphasizing important details, misinterpreting visions/dreams, or saying something the wrong way. I witness these kinds of mistakes frequently. This is why the apostle Paul told both the Corinthian and Thessalonian churches to weigh prophetic words in order to determine what is from God (1 Co. 14:29; 1 Th. 5:21). Accuracy is definitely important, which is why we need to develop prophets so that everyone around them can benefit from a healthy and fruitful prophetic ministry. Don't we do this for people who teach the Scriptures? I have been teaching the Bible for many years, and I can admit that there were times when I confidently proclaimed a truth from Scripture that I later learned I had misinterpreted. I hope we can all agree that those who do such things on purpose are false teachers, but those who do it out of immaturity need encouragement and grace from us as they grow. I believe we need to apply the same principle to prophets that we already employ with those who teach the word of God.

When the Genuine Becomes False

Many years ago, there was well-known itinerant prophet who ministered at a local church in our area. To my knowledge, it was the first and last time that he made his way to Seattle, Washington. People from all over packed out the church with great anticipation. That night he spoke for about thirty minutes and then began to prophesy to various people in the audience. His sermon was fine. His prophetic ministry was accurate. People were encouraged and God was glorified. A couple years later, I heard how this same man had started an online ministry where people called in to receive prophecies for a specific donation. Finding this hard to believe, I went online to research it for myself. What I discovered was far worse than what had been described to me. Searching the ministry's website, I found that you could purchase member subscriptions that included monthly prophetic words. He even sold bars of soap called "prophet soap," which somehow gave you revelation as you washed with it. The worst part was watching one of the online programs in which this prophet actually used astrology as a means of connecting with God. Through all of this, I remember thinking, "How could someone with such a real love for God and such an incredible prophetic ministry fall so far from what he once was?"

It seems unfathomable that something so genuine can become so false, but it happens all the time. There are some who start out following Jesus but take a wrong turn somewhere along the way and end up following themselves, or worse. Some of those people who do this make it clear at times that they are no longer following Jesus, while claiming at other times that what they are doing is from Jesus. Certainly, we could discuss this from a theological perspective as we analyze whether they became an apostate or never were a Christian to begin with.

For our purposes, however, I want to stay focused on the fact that there are people who seem thoroughly Christian and exercise a genuine gift of prophecy who later become false in their ministry. Jesus knows the true state of a person's soul, but we

Jesus knows the true state of a person's soul, but we need to discern when the ministry of an individual becomes false, as well as guard ourselves from that dangerous path.

need to discern when the ministry of an individual becomes false, as well as guard ourselves from that dangerous path.

What causes a person to go down such a dark road? That is a great question! I think the answer is the same for any Christian and not just for those who prophesy. I want to walk through some of the major pitfalls that I have seen turn prophetic voices from fruitful to harmful. Here are a few of the ways that this happens.

1. Offense and bitterness

Like everyone else, prophets can become offended for all kinds of reasons. Maybe their ministry wasn't received or believed in by those around them. Perhaps they were connected to an environment that nurtured other gifts, but not the prophetic, which made them feel overlooked, unneeded, or unappreciated. Regardless of the reason, when offenses are not properly processed through the love and forgiveness of Jesus, bitterness can take root and poison an entire ministry. The writer of Hebrews puts it this way: "See to it that no one comes short of the grace of God; that no root of bitterness springing up causes trouble, and by it many be defiled" (He. 12:15). A root of bitterness growing up in a person's heart can cause "many" to be defiled. Practically speaking, offense and bitterness can cause prophetic people to become harsh and begin focusing on the negative rather than on what God is doing.

2. Envy and jealousy

The sin of jealousy is so powerful that it drove Cain to kill Abel (Ge. 4:8) and Joseph's brothers to sell him into slavery (Ge. 37:28). I have seen prophetic people so desperately desire the level of gifting or platform that another person has that it literally changes who they are. Instead of ministering out of what God has given and working humbly with others, a jealous prophet can be tempted to gossip and conspire against those in the church who possess what they desire.

Ultimately, when this sin is not dealt with, it becomes a distortion to the voice of God and to the discerning capacity of that prophetic person, which brings about terrible fruit that hurts themselves and others.

3. The love of money

Money itself is not evil, but the love of money has the power to corrupt anyone who allows their heart to stray. The Bible actually calls this sin "greed." I have seen prophetic people corrupt their gifting by lying about spiritual experiences and miraculous moments in order to boost their honorariums, speaking invitations, and merchandise sales. They no longer speak the pure word of the Lord because they have compromised their ministry to say what people want to hear, so they can get the money. Prophets who seek profits open themselves up to all kinds of evil. Paul's warning to Timothy is as true today as it was then:

> *But those who want to get rich fall into temptation and a snare and many foolish and harmful desires which plunge men into ruin and destruction. For the love of money is a root of all sorts of evil, and some by longing for it have wandered away from the faith and pierced themselves with many griefs* (1 Timothy 6:9-10).

4. Sexual immorality

Unrepentant sexual immorality in a person's life can open a door to demonic power. I have seen emotionally vulnerable people become attracted to someone because of the prophetic anointing on that person's life. Couple that with a lack of accountability and the basic human sex drive, and we have on our hands a church disaster that has repeated itself time and time again. Those who minister prophetically MUST deal with their sexuality before the Lord or it will corrupt their gifting and lead them down a terrible path.

5. A rebellious heart

One of the clearest signs that a prophetic person is going down the wrong road is a rebellious heart, otherwise known as a lack of submission. I have personally witnessed this problem more than any other. A prideful person who cannot or will not take a humble place under anyone else, unfortunately will experience resistance not only from the church but from GOD HIMSELF (Ja. 4:6; 1 Pe. 5:5). It is easy for prophets and prophetic people to fall into the mental trap of thinking that they know something that nobody else knows, or hear from God in a way nobody else does. Such pride foments rebellion, where submission looks more like compromise than humility, prompting the prideful prophet to label the leader, church, or movement as those who don't follow the voice of God. The saddest part of this is that the prophet becomes hardened and bitter for no reason and ultimately wastes the gifting that God gave to be used for the benefit of the very people the prophet has just labeled.

These are just a few of the ways that I have seen genuine prophets or prophetic people stray from the call of God on their life. It may be that the prophet doesn't fully become false in the sense of no longer being a Christian, but their ministry certainly manifests the same fruit as that of a false prophet. The fact that this happens or is even possible should serve all of us, prophet or not, as a warning from the Lord that our gifts and ministries are from Jesus and require a corresponding character development that looks like Jesus as well.

Recognizing False Prophets

Now that we know what false prophets are and what they are not, how, specifically, do we discern and deal with them in our midst? In the previous section I gave some clear points on how prophets can become false, and those same points will help us in our discernment process. In this section I want to lay out some very clear points that will help us discern well. These points will not always be the case for every false prophet, but they certainly can be, and they will provide a helpful discerning guide for anyone dealing with this personally.

1. False prophets deny Jesus Christ as Lord

Any person who claims to be a prophet but who denies that Jesus is Lord, the Son of God, or part of the Trinity, is certainly a false prophet. The apostle John made it clear that this is the most important way of discerning the true from the false (1 Jn. 4:1-6).

2. False prophets distort the Word of God

Satan lied to Adam and Eve about what God said (Ge. 3:1-7), and false prophets do the very same thing. The apostle Paul told Timothy that the last days would be marked by "deceitful spirits and doctrines of demons" (1 Ti. 4:1). False prophets are usually the mouthpiece and instigators of heretical teachings in the body of Christ. The most obvious heresies either deny the truth of Jesus Christ or the word of God itself. However, I have seen false prophets promote heretical teaching that appeals to the "the lust of the flesh and the lust of the eyes and the boastful pride of life" (1 Jn. 2:16).

3. False prophets practice divination

A false prophet may not use the word divination, but if you ever hear someone reference occultic or new age practices, it is a clear sign that that person's ministry is false. Only God knows the future; therefore, only God can give prophetic words through someone regarding that which is to come. Remember, false prophets function by demonic power, and while demons do not know the future, they do have some knowledge of the past and will often inspire people with supernatural information. There is a massive difference between information and revelation. Psychics, prognosticators, mediums, and new age practitioners receive information from demon spirits. True prophets of the Lord function by revelation given through the Holy

Spirit, and this becomes a key for discernment when dealing with a false prophet (Deut. 18:10; Acts 13:6-10; 16:16-21).

4. *False prophets lead people to follow other gods*

False prophets lead people away from following Jesus to follow themselves or some other god (Deut.13:1-5).

5. *False prophets are self-proclaimed*

False prophets are often quick to refer to themselves as a prophet. They want everyone to know what they have before anyone really knows who they are. Titles such as "prophet" are job descriptions rather than a badge to identify the really spiritual from the less spiritual. When Jesus corrected the church at Thyatira, he said, "But I have *this* against you, that you tolerate the woman Jezebel, who **calls herself a prophetess**" (Rev. 2:20, emphasis added). Jesus wanted this church to see that they had tolerated false prophets in their midst who liked to proclaim themselves as prophets. As I have said previously, I believe that God establishes prophets in the church, but when a person says, "I am a prophet," without the affirmation of the community, it could be a sign of something false that has yet to fully reveal itself.

6. *False prophets say what people WANT to hear*

All of us struggle to some degree with pride and wanting to be noticed, but a false prophet is fueled by it. When Jesus spoke to the crowds in one of His most important sermons, He confronted the promotion of self and the fear of man, both of which are embedded in the very foundation of how a false prophet functions: "Woe *to you* when all men speak well of you, for their fathers used to treat the **false prophets** in the same way" (Lk. 6:26, emphasis added). A true prophet must resist the pressure to say what people want to hear in order to be a reliable voice of what the Holy Spirit is saying.

7. *False prophets have bad fruit in their life*

One of the clearest ways for us to identify false prophets is by examining the substance of their life. Do they have integrity? Do they have a quality relationship with Jesus? Do they treat people with love and respect? Do they submit to authority? Do they honor the word of God? Does their family respect them? Is their home in order? Do they serve in their church? Do they help people? Are they generous? Are they humble? Basically, what I am saying is that a prophet of Jesus should reflect the life and ministry of Jesus. While no prophet is perfect, they also should not look like the opposite of the one they represent, because all of us will be known by the fruit of our life!

> *Beware of the false prophets, who come to you in sheep's clothing, but inwardly are ravenous wolves. You will know them by their fruits. Grapes are not gathered from thorn bushes nor figs from thistles, are they? So every good tree bears good fruit, but the bad tree bears bad fruit* (Matthew 7:15-17).

This list is by no means exhaustive, and not all of these will be the case for every false prophet that we encounter. However, it is important that we realize that in order to truly recognize a false prophet, we have to move beyond this idea that false prophets are just those who give false prophecies. While it is essential that we deal with false prophets and prophecy, we must do so with the utter conviction that *the power and potential of the true prophetic ministry is worth it.*

Chapter 7

The Prophetic Gifts

I hope that by this point you are able to see how the prophetic ministry is more multi-faceted than you might have considered. So far we have looked at the general definition of prophecy, the various kinds of prophets, and the proposition that every Spirit-filled believer can prophesy. However, there remain several very important principles we must discuss that relate to becoming fully equipped to prophesy.

The apostle Paul wrote 13 letters to various churches that he either started or was hoping to visit in the future. In at least three of these letters he addresses the subject of spiritual gifts in great detail (Romans, 1 Corinthians, Ephesians). In his first letter to the Corinthians, Paul identifies nine different gifts or manifestations of the Holy Spirit. Of these nine, I have identified three in particular that are similar to prophecy, and unless we understand the difference, we might assume they are all the same thing.

*Now there are varieties of gifts, but the same Spirit. And there are varieties of ministries, and the same Lord. There are varieties of effects, but the same God who works all things in all persons. But to each one is given the manifestation of the Spirit for the common good. For to one is given the **word of*** *wisdom through the Spirit, and to another the **word of knowledge** according to the same Spirit; to another faith by the same Spirit, and to another gifts of healing by the one Spirit, and to another the effecting of miracles, and to another **prophecy**, and to another the **distinguishing of spirits**, to another various kinds of tongues, and to another the interpretation of tongues. But one and the same Spirit works all these things, distributing to each one individually just as He wills* (1 Corinthians 12:4-11, emphasis added).

The Christians at Corinth were no strangers to spiritual gifts. Paul wrote these words not to instruct the ignorant but to correct and recalibrate those who already were active in this kind of ministry. There are many points to consider from this passage, but here are five that are particularly pertinent to our discussion of the prophetic gifts:

- There are many different spiritual gifts.
- All of the gifts are from the Holy Spirit.
- The same gift can look *somewhat* different in each person.
- All of the gifts, and all of their diversity, *work together* for the common good.
- Some of the gifts are *similar* in nature, but each carry a special focus.

If we were going to build a house, we would need all kinds of tools and materials. The proper relationship between the tools and the materials would be essential if we were going to accomplish such a project. What good is a hammer without nails or wood? A screwdriver without screws? It is obvious that each of these things work together. While all the spiritual gifts work together in some way, there are a few that work together in a specific way just like tools and materials. As we deepen our study of the prophetic ministry, I think it is helpful to define and describe a handful of these spiritual gifts and how they work together because of their relationship to prophecy.

The Word of Knowledge—*Prophetic Hindsight*

A word of knowledge is a specific message with factual information about someone or something that is given supernaturally through the Holy Spirit (1 Co. 12:8). Some translations actually say "message of knowledge," which continues to point out that this gift is a specific word given, not just a general ability for someone to be knowledgeable. I refer to the word of knowledge as "Prophetic Hindsight" because it is a revelation to us about something in the past that we

> **A word of knowledge is a specific message with factual information about someone or something that is given supernaturally through the Holy Spirit (I Co. I2:8).**

did not learn through education, conversation, or any other natural means. While the apostle Paul did not specifically define or describe this gift, we know from many other passages what it looks like when it appears (Jn. 1:47; Acts 5:1-11; 9:10-15; 10:19-23).

It is common for people to mistake a word of knowledge for prophecy because of their similarities; both are supernaturally given and contain specific information. The biggest difference between prophecy and a word of knowledge is that prophecy refers to the present-future while *the word of knowledge refers to the present-past.*

Jesus and His disciples had just left Judea and begun to make their way toward Galilee. There were three different routes they could take to get there, one of which would take them straight through the region of Samaria. It was also the shortest and most direct route. Jews and Samaritans carried a long and deep-seated hostility toward one another; faithful Jews would never travel through Samaria (if possible) for this very reason. Jesus, however, had no problem breaking the cultural barrier because love compelled everything He did.

While traveling through Samaria, Jesus and His disciples stopped to rest at a historic well. The disciples went into the nearby village to buy food while Jesus remained at the well, awaiting their return.

Just then, a Samaritan woman came to draw water from the well, and Jesus engaged her in conversation. This encounter led ultimately to Jesus revealing that He was the Messiah, which he first hinted at by referring to himself as the "water of life" by which people would never thirst again. Here is what happened next:

> *The woman said to Him, "Sir, give me this water, so I will not be thirsty nor come all the way here to draw." He said to her, "Go, call your husband and come here." The woman answered and said, "I have no husband." Jesus said to her, "You have correctly said, 'I have no husband'; for you have had five husbands, and the one whom you now have is not your husband; this you have said truly." The woman said to Him, "Sir, I perceive that You are a prophet"* (John 4:15-19).

This is a beautiful story of Jesus revealing who He is to someone who needed healing from the past and hope for the future. In the midst of this encounter we witness the spiritual gift of the word of knowledge at work in a powerful way. Jesus told the woman factual information about her life that the Holy Spirit revealed to Him. Jesus' knowledge of such personal information about her convinced the woman that He was a prophet. In their world, only prophets could receive such a revelation because only prophets had that kind of anointing. In our world, anyone who is filled with the Spirit can receive words of knowledge like this, which bring the reality of God to the forefront and can change conversations immediately!

One day, I was home alone when someone rang my doorbell. I opened the door to find two guys on my porch who were selling magazines. I welcomed them into my house and bought some magazines, which allowed me the opportunity to share my testimony of meeting Jesus. Neither of them were Christians, but both of them were interested in the supernatural nature of my story. I began to share with them about how we can know God and hear His voice personally. Suddenly, one of them stood up and said "Ah man, we're late; we missed our ride!" I offered them a ride so we could continue our conversation, and they agreed. As we got into my car, the man in my passenger seat asked, "So, how does it work to hear God's voice, then?" Without even thinking about it, I literally said, "Well, for example, when you were 13, you left a loving home, hooked up with a gang, and started running the streets. You went from house to house and things got worse until you finally reached the point of wishing you had never left home. God was reaching out to you through it all to bring you home, and you know this because your mom is a Christian and she reached out to you many times. Is that about right?"

It's hard to describe what happened next, but it started with the man saying to me, "Who in the world are you?" We pulled into the gas station where a van was waiting for them, and the man opened the car door before I could stop and literally ran for the van like he was scared. His friend, who was sitting in the back seat, opened his door, but before getting out, he shook my hand and said with tears in his eyes, "Thank you for everything! I'm not sure what just happened, but we will never forget this."

I would love to tell you that I prayed with those guys to receive Jesus right then and right there, but, unfortunately, that didn't happen. However, the word of knowledge that I shared forced a man to deal with the fact that God is real! God knows everything about everybody, and sometimes He shares a piece of information with us about a person in order to say to them, "I know you!" I have also found that this gift sets the stage for a greater prophetic word by affirming the supernatural nature of the moment. The main thing I love about the word of knowledge is how it reveals the reality of God in a world that is trying to act like He doesn't exist.

The Word of Wisdom–*Prophetic Insight*

A word of wisdom is a specific message that provides a wise strategy or practical application for a current circumstance (1 Co. 12:8). The word of wisdom is not a general impartation from the Holy Spirit to make a person wiser than others, nor is it conventional wisdom itself.

I refer to this gift as 'Prophetic Insight' because it is received like a prophetic revelation but is focused situationally on the present with a clear action step.

Imagine that you are a commander in an army. The scouts have just returned to camp

A word of wisdom is a specific message that provides a wise strategy or practical application for a current circumstance (1 Co. 12:8).

with the report that the enemy armies have set out to attack your city and will be there in just two days. This report has provided you with the knowledge of what has happened, along with the projected war that is soon and coming. The knowledge is helpful. But now you need a plan! You immediately contact your trusted advisors to think through your next steps. A high-ranking officer speaks up and lays out a wise strategy that has all the markings of wisdom and victory, so you make the decision to move forward with his plan. This illustration sheds light on the difference between knowledge and wisdom and what it can look like when you receive a word of wisdom from the Holy Spirit.

Proverbs 25:11 gives a great description of the very nature of this gift: "*Like* apples of gold in settings of silver is a word spoken in right circumstances." In the days of King Solomon, silver was fairly common while gold was quite precious. Essentially, this proverb is saying that "the right word spoken at the right time" is a precious thing in the midst of common circumstances. That is exactly how the word of wisdom functions in our life; it comes as "the right word spoken at the right time."

After the day of Pentecost, the church began to grow, and, as always, with more people come more problems. The Greek-speaking Jews who had come from other nations complained about the native Jews because their widows were being overlooked during the daily food distribution. The apostles of Jesus were made aware of the complaints, but, as they carried such a great burden with the ministry, it was apparent that something new had to be done. It is through this story that we see the word of wisdom released and effective in the body of Christ.

> *"Therefore, brethren, select from among you seven men of good reputation, full of the Spirit and of wisdom, whom we may put in charge of this task. But we will devote ourselves to prayer and to the ministry of the word." The statement found approval with the whole congregation; and they chose Stephen, a man full of faith and of the Holy Spirit, and Philip, Prochorus, Nicanor, Timon, Parmenas and Nicolas, a proselyte from Antioch. And these they brought before the apostles; and after praying, they laid their hands on them* (Acts 6:3-6).

The disciples appointed seven men full of the Spirit and wisdom to oversee the task. The fruit of this strategy brought about total satisfaction for both sides, resulting in the preservation of unity. It seems simple, but that's often how it feels when "the right word is spoken at the right time."

When I married my wife, I became stepfather to her two boys, who had never really known their biological fathers. I fully owned this responsibility and sought to raise them as men of God the best I knew how. My wife and I made a commitment in our home to never speak negative words about their fathers so we could lead our sons through a process of forgiveness. I will never forget the day that one of their fathers contacted us to begin a relationship with his son again. It had been seven years since they had seen each other, so my automatic, non-prayerful response was NO! During that process, the Lord confronted my fears and gave me a word of wisdom regarding our situation. He showed me that I was steering away from something instead of steering toward it, and the word He gave me was, "You need to invite his father in." That is all I heard. As I yielded to the word, it began to unfold in very practical ways, where I invited this man into relationship with his son and our family. I have learned that a word of wisdom can cut through the problems and all of the complicated issues in order to bring the right solution.

For us, this word of wisdom seemed so simple, but became the catalyst for reconciliation in our home.

The Holy Spirit always knows what to do in the midst of the situations we face. Receiving a word of wisdom begins with the acknowledgement that you don't know what to do and you need the Holy Spirit to help. In fact, the book of James tells us that when we lack wisdom, all we have to do is ask God, who gives generously (Ja. 1:5). Like the word of knowledge, the word of wisdom has such similar characteristics to prophecy that it can often be mistaken as the same thing. However, as we continue to learn the differences, I believe we will be more equipped to partner with the Holy Spirit to bring timely words that release insight and strategy.

The Gift of Prophecy–*Prophetic Foresight*

In chapter 2, we nailed down the definition of prophecy as "a message inspired by God communicated through a person." So, what is the gift of prophecy? You may be saying, "Ben, I thought you said that everyone can prophesy, so why are you now saying that only some have the gift of prophecy?" There is a difference, and I want to make this extremely clear, so let's break it down.

— The calling of a prophet

As we have discussed, God calls some people in the body of Christ to be prophets (Eph. 4:11-16). All prophets have the gift of prophecy, as it is a primary function for their ministry.

— The gift of prophecy

Scripture indicates that some of us have the gift of prophecy as more of a resident function (Ro. 12:6). Those who have this gift are not necessarily prophets as we have described, but they do receive and share prophetic words more frequently than others.

— *The anointing to prophesy*

Every believer has the anointing to prophesy because of the out-pouring of the Holy Spirit (Acts 2). However, this does not mean that everyone has the gift of prophecy or the calling of a prophet.

When the apostle Paul wrote to the church at Rome, he sought to encourage the believers toward unity in the midst of diversity. One of the points of diversity carried the simple truth that every member of the body of Christ has a different gift from God:

> *For just as we have many members in one body and **all the members do not have the same function**, so we, who are many, are one body in Christ, and individually members one of another. **Since we have gifts that differ** according to the grace given to us, each of us is to exercise them accordingly: **if prophecy, according to the proportion of his faith**; if service, in his serving; or he who teaches, in his teaching; or he who exhorts, in his exhortation; he who gives, with liberality; he who leads, with diligence; he who shows mercy, with cheerfulness* (Romans 12:4-8, emphasis added).

As you can see, Paul clearly states that all members of the body do not have the same function because each one has a gift that differs from the other. From this passage we can identify that there is a gift of prophecy, but at the same time we know that everyone can prophesy. So, what is the difference, and how do we know if we have the gift?

I know this is a silly illustration, but bear with me here. Think about the faucet in your kitchen sink. In order for the water to flow through it, you need to turn the handle, which opens the valve. In the same way, every Spirit-filled believer can "turn on" the prophetic ability in their life through asking God for a word. We all have the *ability* to flow. However, the difference with those who have the gift of prophecy is that they have the flow without having to "turn on" the handle because prophetic words come to them without asking. In other words, if you find yourself hearing from God for other people consistently without having to ask God for those words, you probably have the gift of prophecy.

The gift of prophecy is "Prophetic Foresight" because it focuses primarily on the present-future. While this may look similar at times to the word of knowledge and the word of wisdom, we know that the primary distinction is the future element. When we prophesy to someone, we are speaking forth the present priorities of God or declaring the desired and determined will of God concerning things in the future. In forthcoming chapters we will dive into how we receive and share prophetic words, but for now I want to be clear about what the gift of prophecy is in light of the truth that all can prophesy.

Discerning of Spirits—*Prophetic Oversight*

The gift of discerning of spirits is the ability to recognize the spiritual source that animates a person, system, or situation (1 Co. 12:10). Essentially, this gift gives us the ability to sense what is going on in the spiritual realm. Sound crazy? Yeah, it's like that sometimes. I refer to this gift as "Prophetic Oversight" because, unlike the other gifts we have discussed, it really deals with the macro picture rather than the specifics.

The gift of discerning of spirits is NOT the ability of general discernment; nor is it the reason that faultfinding Christians criticize everyone (you know what I mean). All Christians must grow in discernment through their study of the Bible and their carefully cultivated relationship with the Lord. However, this gift is meant to bring an overall sense of whether the speech or actions coming from a person or specific situation are animated by the Holy Spirit, a demonic spirit, or a person's soul.

During the several years I spent ministering in various prisons throughout the state of Washington, I worked with a team of people from many different churches, and it was common for us to meet new team members the same day that we went into the prisons to minister. On one of our trips we met up with two new guys who in every way seemed like a great fit for our team. They were knowledgeable, respectful, servant-hearted, and got along with everyone really well. Everything on the outside looked great, but for some reason I had a strong sense that something was "off" with them. After our church services, our whole team drove to a local restaurant for lunch. As we ate, I listened very carefully to everything these two new men said. I had no evidence to think this way, but somehow I could discern that they did not believe that Jesus was God. They never denied the Trinitarian nature of God, and they even signed a doctrinal statement affirming orthodox Christianity, which includes the Trinity. I was seriously torn. When we left the prison, I told the leader of the group what I had felt, and he basically said, "No way!" Although he didn't seem to believe me, I still asked him to have a conversation with these guys before we ministered together again. He said that he would. A few weeks later, the leader of the ministry called me and said, "Well, I don't know how you knew it, but you were right; they don't believe that Jesus is God."

The gift of discerning of spirits is a very powerful and necessary tool in the body of Christ. Here are a few ways that this gift can help us:

- Identify the presence of demonic spirits (Acts 16:16-18).
- Identify unhealthy motivations of a person (Acts 8:18-24).
- Identify the presence or activity of the Holy Spirit (Luke 5:17).
- Avoid deceptive teachings or false prophecy.
- Embrace true prophetic words from the Lord.

I have found that it is easy to misunderstand the discerning of spirits. Just because we sense something is off does not mean that we are free to mistreat people. Demonizing someone shows our immaturity, so it is imperative that we truly seek God for wisdom regarding what to do with what we sense. When the Holy Spirit shows us what's wrong with others, that may also be an invitation for us to be a minister of Jesus to help make wrong things right.

How the Prophetic Gifts Work Together

Our goal in walking through the prophetic gifts is to help us understand and employ the fullness of what the Holy Spirit has made available to us. All of these gifts overlap to some degree because they are all revelatory in nature. However, they each carry something unique and most often work together and even complete each other as we seek the benefit of others.

For example, let's say I am praying for someone and receive a word of knowledge that this person was betrayed by a loved one two years earlier and still has great difficulty trusting people. I then share this word of knowledge with the person and ask if it's true. If this person says, "Yes, that is exactly what I am struggling with!" it is very clear that the Holy Spirit gave me a powerful revelation—but now what? The word of knowledge did a wonderful job opening the door for the next step of ministry. At this point I will ask the Holy Spirit, "What do you want to do?" It could be that I receive a word of wisdom that highlights an action step for this person to take to move beyond the hindrance. I say, "The Lord is prompting you to forgive that person who betrayed you and ask the Holy Spirit to heal you and help you trust again." From there I will pray over the person and then invite him or her to pray into the word of wisdom that I shared. The whole time this has been going on I have been asking the Holy Spirit for a prophetic word, and now He has given it to me. I say, "I believe the Lord has shown me that not only is He going to heal you, but He is going to use your life to bring relational healing and reconciliation to others, starting with your own family!"

In many instances, this is exactly what it looks like to minister to someone prophetically. Can you see how the three different gifts all worked together? The word of knowledge showed me the *past*, the word of wisdom outlined an action step for the *present* and the prophetic word declared what God would do in the unfolding *future*. As I minister to people, I literally think through this as a progressive process to identify what the Holy Spirit is doing. While prophecy often gives the present-future, we now know that a fuller prophetic ministry is available through the prophetic gifts as we pray over people. I encourage you to ask God to show you the *past, present,* and *future* of those that you minister to and then watch what God will do!

Chapter 8

The Purpose of Prophecy

I have been teaching classes and seminars on the prophetic ministry for quite a while. Usually, after each session, I try to reserve some time for questions and answers. This helps me gain an understanding of what people are learning as well what things I may need to refine. During one of our Q & A sessions, one person asked an extremely simple and unassuming question that caused me to pause for a moment: "What is the purpose of prophecy? I mean, what is this really about?" At that moment, for some reason, I didn't have a very good answer.

When you do something for a long time you tend to accept or assume things that others may not fully understand, so it's always good to be brought back to simplicity. The more I thought through the person's question regarding the purpose of prophecy, the more I realized that it cannot be summed up in one statement. In fact, the best way to answer this question may be to say that *prophecy is multi-purposed.*

Prophetic words are like seeds, which, when first planted, all look pretty much the same. But as they grow, they each develop into the type of plant that they truly are. In the same way, all prophetic words sound similar when they are first spoken, but, like a seed, they are planted into someone's heart and have the potential to bear a specific kind of fruit. One prophetic word could bring encouragement while another may release a new sense of freedom. Even though prophetic words are very much multi-purposed, it is important to know that ALL prophetic words carry a common denominator: *The most common purpose of prophecy is to reveal something about God or to release something from God.*

The most common purpose of prophecy is to reveal something about God or to release something from God.

I love prophetic words because of what I have seen them produce in so many different people. Remember, prophetic words are not the flattery of man or the wishful thinking of the sympathetic. Prophetic words are packages from the warehouse of heaven delivered by Spirit-filled postal workers. Each package contains something different because each person has a different need, and the person who receives the word usually is the only one who really knows the purpose for which it was given.

When the apostle Paul gave instructions to the Corinthian church about prophecy, he began his conversation by saying, "Follow the way of love and eagerly desire spiritual gifts, especially the gift of prophecy" (1 Co. 14:1 NIV). Two very clear points from this passage set the tone and trajectory for all prophetic ministry. First, love MUST be the motivation for seeking and sharing prophetic words with people. Second, we are called to "eagerly desire" all spiritual gifts but *especially prophecy*. Does this mean that prophecy is the greatest spiritual gift? Not necessarily. However, I believe that the apostle Paul said this because of the unique benefit that prophecy brings to people when it is healthy and mature (1 Co. 14:3). Do you eagerly desire to prophesy? What's the difference between those who eagerly desire to prophesy and those who don't? One of the major factors that will shift our desire to prophesy into high gear is an experiential knowledge of what prophecy actually does in people's lives.

A few years ago, I was watching television when a commercial from a well-known restaurant came on. Like many restaurant commercials, this one was advertising a special deal on one of their signature dishes. While watching this I had a strange thought: "I wonder how much money they spent on this commercial." For some reason, I felt compelled to find out, and after a few hours of research I concluded that this company could have spent one million dollars for a thirty-second ad that ran for a month. That's right, one million dollars. This number was staggering to me because I couldn't imagine how they were going to get a return on their investment. I am well aware that the people who advertise like this know what they are doing, and nobody would waste this kind of money, so what do they know that I don't know? Well, they definitely believe that if they SHOW you a quality steak dinner repeatedly, it might eventually get you to go to their restaurant. Creating a hunger for something new comes through showing people what they are missing. If you don't see it, then you won't want it. But if you do see it and agree that it's good, then it will create a desire that ultimately leads to action.

This illustration provides some insight into how people eagerly desire the prophetic. You have to see it and experience it in order to desire it. Reading the passage that calls you to eagerly desire prophecy will only tell you that it's important. Witnessing the power of the prophetic, however, will help you understand its purpose and value to the point where you will greatly desire it in your own life. What if "eagerly desiring" prophecy is a way to love people because of the potential fruit that is produced when the gift is shared? For the rest of the chapter I want to walk through the various things that are released when people prophesy, which speak of its purpose beyond a mere definition.

Prophecy Releases Strength

*But everyone who prophesies speaks to men for their **strengthening**, encouragement and comfort* (1 Corinthians 14:3 NIV, emphasis added).

Have you ever found yourself strengthened or encouraged by a prophetic word you received? I sure have. The fact is, words have power.

How much more powerful are words from God? If you are building something and want to make it stronger, you typically have to broaden the structure by adding more material, which makes it more stable and secure. Prophetic words *add something* to people that inspires them to "be strong in the Lord and in the strength of His might" (Eph. 6:10).

Prophetic words add something to people that inspires them to "be strong in the Lord and in the strength of His might" (Eph. 6:10).

Recently, I was driving home from a conference session after a very long night of ministry. I was hungry, so I pulled into the nearest fast food restaurant to get a quick bite to eat. As I ordered my food, the Holy Spirit prompted me to start praying for the man taking my order, so I asked God for a prophetic word. I pulled up and said to the man, "Hello! You don't know me, but sometimes when I pray for people, God gives me a word about their life. This may sound strange, but I believe that God showed me that you recently stepped out of a college counseling program because you didn't have the finances to continue. Is that right?" The man said, "How in the world did you know that?" For the next five minutes I shared my testimony about meeting Jesus— and nobody came through the drive-through the entire time! Before I left, I prayed for this man to know Jesus and prophesied over him that God would provide the finances for him to finish college. As I drove away, I could literally see the strength of God on his face to get back up from a place where he felt defeated.

Prophecy Releases Encouragement

> But everyone who prophesies speaks to men for their strengthening, **encouragement** and comfort (1 Corinthians 14:3 NIV, emphasis added).

The Greek word for encouragement in this verse means to inspire, stimulate, admonish, and sometimes is even translated as "exhortation." God wants to encourage His kids, and one of the ways He does that is by giving us prophetic words for one another. Most people live with a deficit of encouragement; we all need to know that we can do it, that we can make it, and that God is with us. In our church, we set aside some time at the end of worship for myself or one of our prophetic team members to share a corporate prophetic word. During a recent gathering, the Lord showed me a vision for our congregation that released encouragement to many of our people. Here is the word I shared:

> In a vision, I saw someone walking up a large hill. I specifically paid attention to the final stage of their journey, where they made it all the way up to the top. I could tell that it took quite a bit of focus, energy, and time to get all the way up the hill. When the person got to the top, they found nothing more than a barren field. Their countenance dropped and the excitement of reaching this place turned into a depressed frustration almost immediately.

> As I observed this scene a specific word came to my mind. The word was "disillusioned." The word disillusioned means "when one has lost faith or trust in something or someone: to be disappointed that something is not as good, valuable, or true as it had seemed or one had believed it to be."[16] I realized that the vision was a picture of someone who gave a lot of time and effort toward something with great expectation that the outcome would be the opposite of what it actually was. This picture may have been related to a job, a relationship, a habit, or even a ministry. The opposite outcome caused a powerful sense of disillusionment that began to set into their soul, causing discouragement and depression.

> This vision reminded me of John 6 where Jesus had performed powerful miracles in the past like walking on water and the multiplication of food (Jn. 6:1-25). After seeing the miracles, the crowds followed Jesus with great expectation of what might happen next or what they might receive as they followed Him. It was at this point that Jesus called out the crowds for seeking Him because of the miraculous provision. He told them that He was the bread of life, which led to His famous

statement; "He who eats My flesh and drinks My blood abides in Me, and I in him" (Jn. 6:56). After this, MANY in the crowd walked away because they didn't get what they had hoped for. In essence, they were "disillusioned." However, Jesus was speaking the truth by declaring that He was all they needed, and that they must not allow their hope and expectation to be set on SOMETHING rather than SOMEONE.

At this point, Jesus turned around, looked at His disciples, and said "'You do not want to go away also, do you?' Simon Peter answered Him, 'Lord, to whom shall we go? You have words of eternal life'" (Jn. 6:67-68). Peter and the disciples may also have felt discouragement, but somehow they knew what the others did not know: Jesus was the source. It wasn't about the food, the miracles, or the buzz of the crowd—it was about Jesus. It's always about Jesus.

Here is the word prophetic word; We can get let down and disappointed in life. Things don't always work out or go our way. This is not necessarily our fault. However, the Lord would remind us that He is all we truly need. Don't give up—LOOK UP. Don't give in—PRESS IN. Don't walk away—START TO PRAY. Jesus is the source of life and the goal of life. When we have Him, we can always get up and step up. Be encouraged, my friends. God's got you!

Many of the words that release encouragement seem general at first but end up targeting areas of our hearts and inspiring us to greater places. We all try to hold it together on the outside as we go about life, but many of us are carrying deep-seated discouragement. I have watched prophetic words wash away years of discouragement and release new zeal that could only come from the Holy Spirit. May the Holy Spirit pour out prophetic encouragement on us and through us to move forward in Jesus name!

I have watched prophetic words wash away years of discouragement and release new zeal that could only come from the Holy Spirit.

Prophecy Releases Comfort

But everyone who prophesies speaks to men for their strengthening, encouragement and comfort (1 Corinthians 14:3 NIV, emphasis added).

We may never know what the people around us are going through, but there are times when a prophetic word will release comfort beyond anything we could say or do. These kinds of prophetic words bring peace beyond understanding, hope in a seemingly hopeless situation, and faith when our hearts are gripped with fear.

One morning, I was getting ready to preach during a church service. Before I preach I usually pray for about an hour so I can listen to the voice of the Spirit and intercede for people. That morning the Holy Spirit showed me a vision of a woman who was crying for her son, who was in a very difficult place. I asked the Lord about this vision and almost immediately received a word in my heart saying; "Her son's name is Thomas." I began to pray for this woman and her son as if I was going to meet them that morning. Later on, I got up to share my message, but before I did, I shared this word: "During my prayer time this morning I believe the Lord showed me that a woman would be here today who has a son named Thomas. I believe I am to tell you that God is at work in his life and he is going to be okay." After the service, a handful of people thanked me for the sermon, but just as I was about to leave, a woman approached me who had clearly been crying. I asked her how she was doing, and she said, "When you shared that word this morning, did you say that his name was Thomas?" I nodded and said, "Can I show you something?" I opened my journal and showed her what I had written during my time in prayer that morning about her son. Tears began to stream down her face as I spent the next several minutes praying with her for her son Thomas. It was an incredible God moment.

I meet many people who are burdened by life, drowning in difficulty, and just barely holding on. Instead of trying to be everyone's counselor or reciting the usual Christian quips, I ask God for a word that can provide relief where I literally don't know what to say. The truth is, God knows what to say, and His words carry the power to go right into the soul. I picture these words like life preservers that are thrown out on the water of our lives as we are struggling to stay afloat. These words help us stabilize so we can latch on to the promises of Scripture and the character of God, which we know is true in it all and through it all.

Prophecy Releases Confirmation

Since we can all hear the voice of God personally (Jn. 10:27), one of the greatest blessings that prophecy releases is a confirmation of what we are already hearing God say. We can often be uncertain about what we are hearing from God regarding family, career, ministry, or other life decisions. In those moments it is extremely helpful and clarifying when someone gives you a word that matches what you have been praying about. I have personally witnessed and experienced prophetic confirmation on many occasions.

Since we can all hear the voice of God personally (Jn. 10:27), one of the greatest blessings that prophecy releases is a confirmation of what we are already hearing God say.

When the apostle Paul became a Christian, he was told clearly that that he would be used by God to open the eyes of the Gentiles to the person and purpose of Jesus Christ (Acts 9:10-19; 26:14-18). Prior to his first missionary journey, he spent several years at a city called Antioch, along with his friend Barnabas. During a time of prayer and fasting, one of the local prophets gave a word to Paul and Barnabas that became the final confirmation for Paul to launch out into his calling. Paul had already heard this very thing from God, as we have noted, but this word served as an incredible prophetic confirmation in his life.

Now there were at Antioch, in the church that was there, prophets and teachers: Barnabas, and Simeon who was called Niger, and Lucius of Cyrene, and Manaen who had been brought up with Herod the tetrarch, and Saul. While they were ministering to the Lord and fasting, the Holy Spirit said, **"Set apart for Me Barnabas and Saul for the work to which I have called them."** *Then, when they had fasted and prayed and laid their hands on them, they sent them away* (Acts 13:1-3, emphasis added).

I remember a powerful example of confirmation during one of our monthly "Hearing God" meetings. After a time of teaching, I picked someone new out of the crowd, someone I had never seen before. As I prayed for him, I had a vision of a large beach, where I observed him setting up a tent big enough for at least fifty people to sit under. I started to describe the vision to him and, before thinking about it, said, "You and your family are going to plant a church among a diverse community, and God will provide for you and bless you greatly in this!" The man literally laughed out loud in front of everyone. Someone brought him a microphone so he could provide feedback for the word that he received. What happened that night was remarkable. He told us that they had just packed up everything they owned and come to our meeting as a final stop before driving to San Diego, California to plant a church among the beach community. His family had never been to our church before, but recently had been invited, and the only time they could come was that night, on their way out of town.

God is so gracious to give us confirmation in such a profound way. When you ask God for clarity about what He wants you to do, it just may be that you receive that confirmation through a powerful prophetic word!

Prophecy Releases the Reality of God

But if an unbeliever or someone who does not understand comes in while everybody is prophesying, **he will be convinced** *by all that he is a sinner and will be judged by all, and* **the secrets of his heart will be laid bare.**

*So he will fall down and worship God, exclaiming, "**God is really among you!**" (1 Corinthians 14:24-25 NIV, emphasis added)*

In this chapter, the apostle Paul clarified the proper application of spiritual language and the gathered importance of the prophetic gift. When prophecy is released in a healthy way, the outcome is revolutionary for those who don't know God or haven't experienced his power. I have spent many hours trying to explain who Jesus is to those who don't believe in Him. Answering questions, listening to the criticism, advocating the authority of the Bible; I have done all of that and I will always continue to do so. However, I love the moments when God gives me a prophetic word for someone who doesn't follow Jesus and they can't say anything except, "God is really among you!"

One day, I was invited to minister at an outdoor festival a few hours away from where I live. I drove up to the event and joined with the crowd as I waited for my time to preach. After my message, I walked across the street to my car and passed by two city employees who were hired to oversee the parking lot. Just as I walked by, I heard the Holy Spirit say, "Go back and talk to them!" I took a few more steps and stopped. I turned around, walked up to them, and said, "Hey guys, how are you doing?" They both looked at me and said, "Fine, I guess." I literally had nothing to say, so I started stalling as I waited on the Holy Spirit. Just then I looked at the man on the right and said, "I believe that God just showed me that your sister is in the hospital because she overdosed this weekend. You and your family have been vexed by this news, but I want you to know she is going to pull through." The second guy literally said out loud, "What the ____!" The other man said to me, "How did you know that?" I spent the next 5 minutes sharing my testimony about meeting Jesus and about how much He loved them. I asked these guys if I could pray with them for his sister, and before saying yes they took off their hats to honor the moment. I prayed for them, encouraged them, and prophesied over their families. That day, those guys walked away saying, "God is real and He is surely among you!" The reality of Jesus was released in their lives, and there is no way that they will ever forget it.

In a culture of philosophy and debate, the apostle Paul made it clear that "the kingdom of God is not a matter of talk but of power" (1 Co. 4:20 NIV). Our culture has striking similarities to the one in which Paul ministered, and one of the manifestations of God's power among us is released in the form of prophetic words. When the reality of God is revealed to someone, they are convicted by the truth and forced to make a decision to either surrender to God or harden their heart. No matter what choice they make, there is no going back to life as usual when God shows up through a supernatural prophecy.

When the reality of God is revealed to someone, they are convicted by the truth and forced to make a decision to either surrender to God or harden their heart.

Prophecy Releases Direction

I can't tell you how many times I have heard someone say, "Prophecy *ONLY* confirms what you are already hearing from God yourself." I definitely share the underlying sentiment of this statement, but if we are going to imply that God *only* gives prophetic confirmation, then we must have a very clear Bible verse that actually says that. Guess what? We don't! That said, I don't think that the primary way the Holy Spirit brings us direction is through a prophetic word, but it certainly does happen at times. It could be that you have a wrong view of who you are and therefore disqualify yourself from a future assignment. Your ears may be closed to future possibilities, so God in His grace sends a prophetic word your way to cause you to reconsider what you so easily dismiss. I am sure that there are other reasons for God giving prophetic direction, but in my experience, this seems to be the most frequent.

While I do believe there are times where God gives prophetic words that highlight future direction we haven't heard yet, I still think we need to be careful. When someone tells me what is going on in their life and then asks me for a directional prophetic word, I usually just say NO! That is not the way it works. We cannot seek a prophetic word in place of cultivating our own relationship with God. Additionally, I am quite specific with anyone in our circle about not giving prophetic words regarding a spouse, children, or specific dates. I am not saying that God doesn't give these kinds of words at times, but those occasions are few and far between. If it does happen, we make sure to submit it in a manner that a person can weigh it without feeling any unnecessary pressure.

I have already shared my story of receiving a prophetic word about writing books. I had never considered writing books before hearing this word, and yet, here I am. I remember giving a prophetic word to a woman about starting a ministry to bring healing and restoration to women, and she responded, "Okay, I am not sure about that." This same woman is now responsible for starting several ministries that focus their efforts on reaching women on the streets and also in strip clubs! If you are ever given a prophetic word that doesn't serve as a confirmation, simply take it to the Lord and ask if this is His direction for your life. There is no need to be concerned, because God will confirm it to you if it is truly for you.

Prophecy Releases Correction

God corrects us because He loves us and wants the very best for our lives. The word "correction" simply means to set right again, to make paths straight, to rebuke, or to point out error. Although we are born again and made new by God's Spirit, not all of our mind is renewed yet (Ro. 12:1-2); thus, not all of our choices are of God. Therefore, we need God's loving and Fatherly voice of correction to reveal the right way, in contrast to what we may be thinking or doing.

The Bible is the primary voice of God in our lives, and we clearly see that one of the main purposes of Scripture is to provide correction in order to shape us: "All Scripture is inspired by God and profitable for teaching, for reproof, **for correction**, for training in righteousness; so that the man of God may be adequate, equipped for every good work" (2 Ti. 3:16-17, emphasis added). The correction aspect of Scripture is important so we can move away from what's wrong and step into what's right. The goal of God's correction is not just to make us feel bad for the wrong, but to help us live in who He really created us to be. From this we can clearly see that God brings correction into our lives; the only question is whether or not he will do it through a prophetic word.

In the Old Testament, God regularly gave the prophets corrective words for people or nations that carried consequences of blessing for obedience and judgment for disobedience. In the New Testament, as we have already seen, the primary nature of prophecy is to edify, encourage and comfort (1 Co. 14:3). While I certainly agree that the typical prophetic word is not corrective in nature, I still think that it happens, and we must learn how to handle these kinds of words.

There is a clear pattern for giving corrective prophetic words in the book of Revelation. The apostle John wrote the book of Revelation from a series of visions and prophetic words that he received from God (Rev. 1). In chapters two and three, John writes to seven churches throughout Asia Minor and speaks to all of them in a similar way. The prophetic pattern goes like this: he commends them for what they are doing well, he corrects them for what they are doing wrong, and he exhorts them toward true repentance, with corresponding consequences. If we are going to see any fruit from corrective prophecy, we must practice it in the same way.

Like many others, I have seen people give corrective and warning prophecies that have released harm and confusion. This is why some churches and ministries don't allow anybody to give corrective prophecy whatsoever. I understand that. I believe that God's primary way of bringing correction to His people is first through relationship and, secondarily, through leadership (Mt. 18). However, in a healthy prophetic culture, we can grow in our ability to receive and release the fullness of God's heart, which may involve setting something right in a correctional sense.

If we are going to allow correctional words, then we must build clear parameters and train people to minister in them so we can truly hear and heed the word of the Lord. First of all, correctional prophetic words are not the same as judgment words that we read about in the Old Testament. The prophetic word cannot be, "Here is what you are doing wrong, and if you don't repent, judgment is at hand!" When the apostle John conveyed the prophetic words from Jesus in the book of Revelation, he did not speak the correction without the commendation. When people give a correctional prophetic word,

When people give a correctional prophetic word, it must be clear and convey a hope for what God wants to do.

it must be clear and convey a hope for what God wants to do. Additionally, we should require prophetic people to have a proper perspective of the good alongside their correction. These kinds of safeguards will not only ensure health for those receiving the words, but also for those who give them. As we welcome and establish the prophetic ministry, we must do so in a way that is available to any kind of word that God may give, including those that carry correction.

Chapter 9

Receiving Prophetic Words from God

In my first book, *Hearing God,* my goal was to convince everyone that God communicates to all of us personally. My goal in this second book is to build on that concept, because once you believe that God speaks to you personally, it is much easier to believe that He will speak through you prophetically. The transition is seamless. The fact is that we receive prophetic words for others the same way we hear the voice of God for our own lives. The critical question is, How familiar are you with the way the Holy Spirit communicates to you? God is speaking to us all the time, but we may not always discern the way in which He is communicating because seldom is God's voice an actual voice.

We live in a world that uses multiple forms of communication. It's highly probable that everyone reading this book uses two, three, or even more forms of communication on an everyday basis. We could talk about sign language, braille, emails, text messages, emojis, and, of course, "old-fashioned" telephone voice communications. Additionally, there are more than 6,500 different languages spoken in our world, and that doesn't even include body language, which can be just as powerful (and all the married people say AMEN!). In a similar way, God uses many forms of communication with us and we need to understand these if we are to regularly receive prophetic words for others.

Most books on the prophetic ministry highlight a specific process of revelation, interpretation, and application. Obviously, receiving prophetic revelation is the most important part of this process, because in order to give a prophetic word to someone, you first must receive it from God. Throughout the remainder of this chapter, I am going to walk us through the various ways that God speaks to us prophetically. By sharing these I am in no way saying that they are the only ways that God communicates, but I have found them to be more common in my experience, and, most importantly, in Scripture.

Receiving Prophetic Words from the Bible

The primary way that we hear and discern the voice of God begins and ends with the Bible. The Bible is infallible and contains the general will of God, which never changes, for every believer in every generation. God's infallible Word is always the first place we go to hear from God, and it is the first place we go to discern what we believe the Holy Spirit might be saying to us. With this in mind, I encourage you to consider the priority you place on the Bible in your daily life, because it truly makes a difference.

Toward the end of his life, the apostle Paul wrote a letter to his son in the faith, Timothy. The truths that he wrote were extremely important, especially because they were some of the final things that he would ever say. Paul wanted Timothy to understand that the Bible was "inspired," or, more literally, "God-breathed"; therefore, the books contained therein have divine power to transform lives. The apostle Peter also wrote with the same notion to his readers, that Scripture is not a product of human will or imagination, but rather, "inspired" by the Holy Spirit

*All Scripture is **inspired** by God and profitable for teaching, for reproof, for correction, for training in righteousness; so that the man of God may be adequate, equipped for every good work* (2 Timothy 3:16-17, emphasis added).

*But know this first of all, that no prophecy of Scripture is a matter of one's own interpretation, for no prophecy was ever made by an act of human will, but men **moved by the Holy Spirit spoke from God*** (2 Peter 1:20-21, emphasis added).

For many years now, my daily practice has been to read and study God's Word. Additionally, I have learned to journal my thoughts, observations, questions, and any unique passages that stand out for me. Something I have discovered through the practice of this discipline is how the Holy Spirit often will highlight verses of Scripture during my personal time of devotion that are meant for me to share with someone else during the day. While this is not my primary motivation for spending time in God's Word, it has certainly become a normal way that I receive prophetic words for people.

One day, when I was reading the Bible as I normally do, a few verses from Mark 6 stood out for me, so I wrote them down:

The apostles gathered together with Jesus; and they reported to Him all that they had done and taught. And He said to them, "Come away by yourselves to a secluded place and rest a while." (For there were many people coming and going, and they did not even have time to eat.) They went away in the boat to a secluded place by themselves (Mark 6:30-32).

As I pondered these verses, I received a powerful revelation of the importance of rest and intimacy with Jesus amidst the busyness of ministry. I wrote down many observations that spoke to my heart, but all of them were personal, without even a thought that they might be prophetic for someone else. Later that day, I was in a moment of prayer for one of my friends who is also a pastor. While I was praying, the Holy Spirit reminded me of the passage of Scripture that I had been pondering that morning. Somehow I knew that this verse was prophetic for my friend, so I called him right then and said, "Hey, man, I was just praying for you and a Scripture came to my mind from Mark 6." I then proceeded to read the whole passage to him. My friend sounded really surprised and asked me, "Have I talked to you in the last week?" I assured him that we had not talked for several weeks. For the next ten minutes my friend told me that the Holy Spirit had spoken the very same Scripture to him a week earlier, which had prompted him to ask his church council for a three-month sabbatical. He was overwhelmed by this prophetic confirmation, and we both praised God together for His voice in our lives!

Receiving Prophetic Impressions

An impression is an internal sense where you feel, think, or know something regarding a person or a situation. There are no direct references to the word "impression" in the Bible, mainly because this word is meant to describe various experiences that seem common to many. One instance where I think an impression makes an appearance in the Bible is found in Acts 27. The apostle Paul had been imprisoned for some time, and, in the process of this ongoing situation, he had appealed to stand trial before Caesar. Shortly after making his appeal, Paul was sent to Rome by ship to present his case to the Emperor. The voyage was plagued by stormy weather, contrary winds, and rough seas. In the midst of it all, the Lord gave Paul a prophetic impression of what was going to happen:

> *When considerable time had passed and the voyage was now dangerous, since even the fast was already over, Paul began to admonish them, and said to them, "**Men, I perceive that the voyage will certainly be with damage and great loss, not only of the cargo and the ship, but also of our lives.**" But the centurion was more persuaded by the pilot and the captain of the ship than by what was being said by Paul* (Acts 27:9-11, emphasis added).

Prophetic impressions will come either as an internal sense or an actual physical feeling. The majority of the impressions that I receive are internal, but at times I experience a physical feeling of some kind that prompts me to pray or prophesy. For example, I was preaching at a church one evening, and during my mes-

Prophetic impressions will come either as an internal sense or an actual physical feeling.

sage I kept feeling a physical pain in my neck. The pain reached the point where I needed to do something, so I asked out loud, "Does anybody have a serious neck pain on the right side that is causing you difficulty right now?" A woman in the back of the room immediately stood up. "That's me, she said, and proceeded to describe for us the rest of her physical condition. We stopped the service right then and there and began to pray for her. She came to church the next morning to give a testimony of the healing power of Jesus: she had slept peacefully all through the night and no longer had any pain. Since her condition had plagued her for several years, she was ecstatic and couldn't stop telling everybody!

On another occasion, I was attending a retreat and several young men walked over to me and we started a conversation. As I simply looked at one of the guys, I immediately sensed an overwhelming feeling of loss. A few moments later, I began to prophesy to this young man. "I sense that you have experienced great loss, but God wants you to know that He is with you and will use your life to impact people who have also gone through similar trauma." This word deeply impacted the young man, because he had recently lost a family member to suicide. The entire experience started with a simple impression that opened up a prophetic moment that will not easily be forgotten. The more we step out and employ what we think God is saying to us, the easier it becomes to determine the accuracy of the prophetic impressions we receive.

Receiving Prophetic Thoughts

Another important way that God speaks to us prophetically is through our thoughts. For me, this will happen in very normal moments, such as when I am driving down the road. All of a sudden, a thought will pop into my mind: "How is John doing?" The thought sounds a lot like my own voice, and most of the time I think it's just a random thought about a person I haven't seen for a while. If I decide to call John, however, more times than not, it turns out that my phone call was timely and extremely prophetic as we talk and pray about something he is going through. Has this ever happened to you?

God cares about everything in our life, even the small stuff. I can't tell you how many times I have lost or misplaced my keys or phone, and as I frantically search through my house, I start to pray, "God, please show me where my keys are." Guess what happens not long after that prayer? That's right! A thought pops into my mind that reveals the last place I put my keys or phone. God speaks into our thoughts a lot more than we may realize, and as we learn to ask Him for prophetic thoughts toward others, we will surely experience an increase.

The Bible has a lot to say about our minds. Paul tells us plainly that "we have the mind of Christ" (1 Co. 2:16). In other words, as we are born of the Spirit, we are born to think the way Jesus does, and it's reasonable to assume that there will be a consistent flow of God's thoughts streaming into our mind. This doesn't mean that everything we think is a prophetic word from God. But it does mean that God has permanent access to our mind and will speak into our thoughts more regularly than we might realize. This, of course, leads us to a very important conclusion that we can expound upon: *not every thought that comes into our mind is our own*. Most of our thoughts are just the direct result of a healthy, functioning brain, while other thoughts are from the Lord, and some even come from a demonic source. This truth will help us as we discern through the flow of thoughts in order to receive from the Lord in our daily life.

There are several Scriptures that reference "God's thoughts" in one way or another. At one point King David speaks of God's thoughts toward us: " Many, O LORD my God, are the wonders which You have done, **And Your thoughts toward us; There is none to compare with You. If I would declare and speak of them, They would be too numerous to count** (Ps. 40:5, emphasis added). As we ask God for prophetic words for others, one way to pray might be, "God, would you show me the thoughts that you have toward John?" In response to this, the Holy Spirit will reveal the heart and mind of the Father toward John, which become the seeds of our prophetic word.

Receiving Prophetic Visions

When the Holy Spirit was poured out on the Day of Pentecost, the apostle Peter stood up to explain what was taking place by quoting a prophecy from the book of Joel:

> *"AND IT SHALL BE IN THE LAST DAYS," God says, "THAT I WILL POUR FORTH OF MY SPIRIT ON ALL MANKIND; AND YOUR SONS AND YOUR DAUGHTERS SHALL PROPHESY, AND YOUR YOUNG MEN SHALL SEE VISIONS, AND YOUR OLD MEN SHALL DREAM DREAMS; EVEN ON MY BONDSLAVES, BOTH MEN AND WOMEN, I WILL IN THOSE DAYS POUR FORTH OF MY SPIRIT And they shall prophesy"* (Acts 2:17-18).

Prophetic visions were not new to the people that Peter was talking to. However, what was new to them was the idea that anybody could receive from the Holy Spirit in the same way as the prophets of old. Peter declared that the prophecy of Joel was now being fulfilled, which would result in the Holy Spirit being poured out. The evidence of this new Holy Spirit reality would be the release of dreams, visions, and prophecy through the common believer. This is truly amazing, and exactly why I believe that every Christian can prophesy!

What exactly is a vision? A vision is where the Holy Spirit opens your spiritual eyes to see something He is doing or is about to do. The Bible references many visions in both the Old and New Testaments. Prophetic visions can be literal, which means that the thing you see is going to happen just as you saw it (Acts 16:9-10). They can also be symbolic, which will require an interpretation from the Holy Spirit in order to understand and convey the message (Acts 10:9-16).

> **A vision is where the Holy Spirit opens your spiritual eyes to see something He is doing or is about to do.**

Prophetic visions are typically received in two different ways. The first is *internally*. Usually this happens as you are praying, maybe even with your eyes closed; you will see a collection of pictures or something like a movie clip in your mind. This tends to be the normal way I receive a prophetic vision, which makes sense when you consider that the Holy Spirit lives in you. The second way you may receive a prophetic vision is *externally*, commonly referred to as an "open vision." An open vision is where God opens your physical eyes to see something in the spiritual realm. A classic example of an open vision is where Elisha asked God to open the eyes of his servant to see the angelic armies in the spiritual realm (2 Ki. 6:17).

Through facilitating many training seminars, I have found that an overwhelming majority of people receive prophetic visions as they pray for people. This can be the case even for those who are prophesying for the first time. During my most recent prophetic training, I was asked to demonstrate how to prophesy, so I began to pray for a woman in our group whom I had never met before. As I waited on the Lord, I received a vision that had two separate scenes. During the first part of the vision, I saw her in the backyard of a home and she was helping her friend fix a fence that had been damaged. In the second part of the vision, I saw her inside a house and she was helping her friend fix parts of the home, as well as redecorate. Once the vision ended, I described it to her just as I saw it and then said, "The Lord sees you and wants to encourage you that through the big and small things your heart is to serve and this is how you impact the lives of people around you!" She thanked me for what I had shared, and while everyone else was talking, she told me that within the past few weeks she had LITERALLY done the exact things I had described. This was a literal vision that I saw internally, and it was exactly what this woman had been doing.

The Lord is pouring out prophetic visions, and all you have to do is ask Him to open your eyes. As you ask the Lord, wait on Him and take note of the things that come to your mind. So often we think that the pictures and video clips that come to our mind are nothing more than our imagination. What if part of the reason that God gave us our imagination is for the purpose of being a prophetic people? One thing is for sure; as God pours out His Spirit, we will see visions!

Receiving Prophetic Dreams

Most of us spend close to one-third of our entire life in sleep. Think about that for a moment. God created us in such a way that we need to power down once a day so that our body can rest and replenish itself. With the abundance of references to dreams in the Bible, it is my conviction that God wants to use our sleep time to communicate with us. And He does that through dreams.

Dreams are very similar to visions, except for the obvious fact that you are asleep. Both visions and dreams can be literal or symbolic, which means interpretation may be required to understand the message that God is trying to convey. I have found that a large percentage of dreams from God tend to be for the individual who had the dream. God may give you a dream that is a prophetic word *for* you but not always intended to be a prophetic word *through* you.

Additionally, I have noticed that most people who receive prophetic dreams for others are usually prophets, or at least carry a high-level prophetic gifting.

I have experienced a handful of significant God-given dreams. In the beginning of 2004, I was a youth leader for a small church in Kirkland, Washington. One night I dreamed that I was sitting in the back of a medium-sized church during an evening service. I was familiar with the church and had even attended for 3-6 months prior to joining this church plant. The worship had just finished, and one of the pastors stood up and began to share announcements. When the pastor finished the announcements, he introduced the guest speaker for the evening, mentioning also that the speaker was a new staff member at the church. As he began to describe the speaker, I realized he was actually talking about me. I looked down in my lap, and there was my Bible, with some notes crammed in the middle; yet, I still was in shock as to what was happening. I walked up to the front of the church, put my Bible and notes on the podium, and cleared my throat. As I began to speak, all that I could say was, "God loves you, and He wants you to spend time with Him; this is what He wants." After the third time of saying this, I sensed the strong presence of the Holy Spirit, and people everywhere began to weep and repent out of sincere love for God. It was a powerful moment.

Just a few months after this dream, our church in Kirkland closed its doors and the people dispersed into other churches. My wife and I tried to attend other churches, but I could not let go of the dream that I had received. After a few months, we settled into the church that was in my dream, and I pursued a career in real estate to provide for my family. We began serving in the church, but my work was requiring most of my time, so I pretty much forgot about the dream entirely. Approximately 7 years later, the Senior Pastor asked me if I would consider a pastoral position at the church. Initially, I was hesitant; however, after remembering the dream I was given, I accepted the position. As I am writing this book today, I am still on staff at that same church! The awesome thing about the dream, at least on the fulfillment side of it, is that I knew now what the Lord was trying to tell me. He was sharing with me that I was called to encourage the church into a closer walk with Jesus, and I think that has pretty much been true of my ministry. This dream was a prophetic word for my life that I received 7 years before it actually happened. That sometimes is how prophetic dreams work.

As we look at Scriptures regarding dreams, we find a few common categorical themes that I think will help us when God speaks to us this way. First, dreams can often be *directional.* **A directional dream is** Most of the dreams I receive **where God shows you** from God are directional in **where He wants you to** nature. A directional dream **go or what He wants you** is where God shows you **to do.** where He wants you to go or what He wants you to do. A good example of a directional dream is found in the story surrounding the birth of Jesus Christ:

> *Now when they had gone, behold, an angel of the Lord appeared to Joseph in a dream and said, "Get up! Take the Child and His mother and flee to Egypt, and remain there until I tell you; for Herod is going to search for the Child to destroy Him." So Joseph got up and took the Child and His mother while it was still night, and left for Egypt. He remained there until the death of Herod. This was to fulfill what had been spoken by the Lord through the prophet: "OUT OF EGYPT I CALLED MY SON"* (Matthew 2:13-15).

Shortly after Jesus was born, God gave Joseph a dream to tell him where to go so that Jesus would be protected from King Herod. This was not the first time that God had spoken to Joseph in a dream, so it may be worth noting that God will establish a pattern of directional dreams if and when He chooses to speak to you this way.

The second category of dreams we see in Scripture are *correctional* dreams. A correctional dream is meant to prevent you from continuing in a certain direction or sin that is harming you, your relationship with God, and, quite possibly, other people around you. In the book of Job we find an interesting passage that gives insight into what I call correctional dreams.

> *Indeed God speaks once, Or twice, yet no one notices it. In a dream, a vision of the night, When sound sleep falls on men, While they slumber in their beds, Then He opens the ears of men, And seals their instruction, That He may turn man aside* from *his conduct, And keep man from pride; He keeps back his soul from the pit, And his life from passing over into Sheol"* (Job 33:14-18).

This passage reveals how God may use dreams to impart instruction, turn us from our current choices, or keep us from pride, and in so doing save us from destruction. If other means of communicating with us are not working, God may use a dream to bring about correction. I have received clear correction from the Lord in a dream a handful of times. Correction is such an important part of our development and necessary to help us to stay on the right path.

The third category of dreams we may experience are *prophetic* dreams. In a prophetic dream, God shows us something that will happen in the future for someone else. In a sense, all dreams are prophetic, but specifically "prophetic dreams" are those which become a prophetic word through us and not for us. While the majority of dreams in the Bible are related to the individual having the dream, there are a handful of prophetic dreams as well (Daniel 7).

The three categories of dreams that I suggested are not the only kinds of dreams that God gives, but I have found them to be the most common in Scripture. As we close the conversation on dreams, I need to issue a warning. I have seen so many people get too caught up in the details and obscure pieces of some dream they feel is from the Lord. Please hear me: God is not playing some cosmic game with us where He wants to see if we can put the obscure puzzle together. When a dream is not clear, and needs interpretation, then the only one who can interpret the dream is the same one who gave it—God. Let's remember what Joseph said when he was asked to interpret Pharaoh's dream when nobody else could: "Joseph then answered Pharaoh, saying, 'It is not in me; God will give Pharaoh a favorable answer'" (Ge. 41:16). The interpretation belongs to God and He will reveal what He is trying to say to us as we seek Him. If God doesn't reveal the answer to you as you pray, don't stress about trying to figure it out; just be patient and wait for His answer.

Receiving God's Prophetic Voice

There are times when God bypasses every other form of communication and simply allows us to hear His voice as an actual voice. The majority of Scripture speaks of the voice of God as an audible voice. I have read many books and listened to several testimonies from people who claim to have heard the audible voice of God. Although I have experienced many supernatural things, I have never heard God's audible voice personally. I don't doubt for a second that some people have, but so far, I am not one of them. I don't believe that hearing the audible voice of God is a typical prophetic experience as we minister to people, so I am not going to focus much on it in this section. That said, there is another way that we hear the prophetic voice of God, which I call the *internal voice* of the Holy Spirit.

Sometimes we will hear God speak to us in our heart, and it very much comes across as a voice rather than just our own thoughts. As we have discussed, the Holy Spirit lives inside of us, which is why hearing His "internal voice" will be more common than His "audible voice." You may have heard others refer to this kind of communication as the "still small voice" of God, or maybe even relate this to the human conscience. Either way, we are really talking about the same thing.

One of our missionaries came to our church once to preach during our weekend services and touch base with our congregation about what God was doing in their ministry. As he was preaching, I literally heard a voice say, "January 21" in the middle of his message. It was so clear that I knew it was the Holy Spirit, and I had to share it with him even though I had no idea what it meant. After the service, we were both busy and I wasn't able to get to him, so I sent him a message saying that I had received a date while he was preaching but I didn't know what it meant. We didn't discuss what it could mean, so I just left it to him to discern. About a year later, I heard a crazy story about how this prophetic date encouraged their faith in something very specific. The year they came to our church, they had been looking for a building, but because of the area they live in, they couldn't get a lease. Many months went by as they approached the new year, and the Lord reminded them of the date I had shared. They began to pray into it, believing that God was doing something, and, finally, they secured a new facility. A funny detail was that they secured the lease on January 22 in their country, but because they are many hours ahead, it was still January 21 in my country. Although this didn't seem like much of a prophetic word to me at the time, it really became something profound to them in the midst of their circumstance.

When God speaks to me this way, I usually hear clear words, phrases, or sentences that speak right into an issue of someone's life. Typically, as I pray for someone, I hear the internal voice of the Holy Spirit in my heart, which sounds like, "Tell Sam that I will provide finances if he takes the next step." The internal voice of the Holy Spirit will always be addressed to you, not as you, which will be a primary key in discerning that it is God and not just your own thoughts. You will typically hear things like, "Tell Ben this ...", "My Word says ..." or "Encourage her to read Psalm 91." This type of communication does not require interpretation, although the way

The internal voice of the Holy Spirit will always be addressed to you, not as you, which will be a primary key in discerning that it is God and not just your own thoughts.

that you minister the word to someone may require sensitivity depending on what the word is (more on that in the next chapter).

Receiving a Prophetic Flow

So far we have discussed the different ways that we receive prophetic words from the Holy Spirit prior to prophesying. However, there is another aspect of receiving prophetically from God that has less to do with getting a word in advance and more to do with receiving the anointing to prophesy. There are times when I literally have nothing in my mind or heart, and as I begin to prophesy over someone, the words start to flow. It's almost like stepping into a river and the water of God's anointing begins to flow through you in a very normal way.

When I talk about receiving a prophetic flow, I am really referring to ministering in the anointing of the Holy Spirit. I believe this experience is referenced in the Bible, where the Holy Spirit rested upon people and they prophesied (Nu. 11:25; Acts 19:6). Walking in a prophetic flow requires great faith as you step out and minister to people, so I don't advise this kind of risk for those who are just beginning to prophesy. I was probably ministering prophetically for five to seven years before I realized that this is something that the Holy Spirit does.

A few years ago, I was invited to a new church down south that I had never been to. After teaching, I chose a few people in the audience to pray for, and in that moment I had nothing in my mind for anyone. I pointed to someone in the back who I did not know, and as I began to prophesy, here is what happened, from his personal testimony:

In March of 2017, Ben came to our church and gave me a prophetic word. He told me that God was opening a door at work and answering some specific prayers that I had been praying regarding corporate management noticing my dedication to the company and the successful completion of many challenges. For some background; I was the Service Manager for the local branch at the time and I took on many tasks that were outside of my job description. I would sometimes "take the blame" for things that were not really my fault, so others would not suffer. Ben specifically said that, "Some have not done right by you, and God is not going to make it alright, but will make your heart alright." I believe this part of the prophecy was related to those situations. Ben prophesied that in April of 2017, I would begin to see the door opening at work. In the beginning of June 2017, my regional manager was in the branch one day and said he needed about 30 minutes alone with me. I assumed that it was another project that I needed to complete. He took me to breakfast and told me that because I had completed every challenge that had been given to me, and completed them well, he wanted to offer me the corporate position of Director of Training for the entire company, which consists of 13 branches and about 250 employees. It was not until June that I was offered the position, but my name had been being discussed for the position since April, which is when Ben had prophesied a door at work would open!

As you can see, this prophetic word and its fulfillment are entirely supernatural. I remember that night specifically. The Holy Spirit released a prophetic flow that was activated by the faith to step out and prophesy, even though I had no pre-planned words to share. Cultivating a prophetic flow takes years of ministry experience and connection with the Holy Spirit, but it can be some of the most powerful prophetic moments that you will ever see.

Chapter 10

Learning How to Prophesy

I must admit, when I first began to prophesy, I didn't have any guidelines, coaching, practical principles, or even much encouragement to do so. And, as you can imagine, the words that I shared were probably not what they could have and should have been. But that's what learning is all about. You just don't know what you don't know, so you have to start with what you have!

This may have been the way I started in the prophetic ministry, but that doesn't have to be the case for everyone else. Sure, we all have to learn through trial and error to some degree. However, some errors are unnecessary and easily avoided if we have the right information, a teachable heart, and the tenacity to keep growing. Trust me; I have seen it done better, in a shorter amount of time, and with a greater outcome than what I experienced. This is why I am passionate about helping people learn to prophesy. If we are going to do this, we must do it well, and to do it well requires that we implement a process of learning that sets the right trajectory.

I am a little embarrassed to admit it, but I have a thing for nice watches. I really like watches, and I can't even explain why. I just do. That said, I may or may not have a couple of nice watches in my possession, but in an attempt to protect the guilty, I can neither confirm nor deny this accusation. What I do know for sure is that when you buy an expensive watch, it comes in a very nice box. The package the watch comes in speaks about the quality of the watch itself. In a similar way, a prophecy is a precious and costly blessing that should come with the kind of presentation that represents the value and importance of what is being given.

Nobody starts out in any gift with the best presentation. In fact, most of us are somewhat embarrassed by our earliest attempts at sharing the gospel, preaching a sermon, or giving a prophetic word. This is why we must stress the importance of learning to prophesy so that we can present the beauty of a prophetic word without all of the unnecessary baggage that turns so many people off. I prophesy regularly, and I have a high tolerance for people making mistakes, but there are some mistakes that aren't even addressed in most churches, which makes it hard for the prophetic to become a normal part of what we do in community.

The apostle Paul, writing to the church at Rome, encouraged them to value one another and the different gifts that they all had been given by God. When it came to the gift of prophecy, he made a comment that I believe is important to emphasize as we are learning to prophesy:

> *Since we have gifts that differ according to the grace given to us, each of us is to **exercise them** accordingly: **if prophecy, according to the proportion of his faith*** (Romans 12:6, emphasis added).

As you can see here, Paul encouraged each person to "exercise" their gift. The word exercise implies that we put something into practice; we actually "do it." His purpose for writing this was not merely to explain that there are many different gifts. Paul sought to encourage the people of God to "exercise" the gift they had been given, no matter what it was. This leads us to an extremely important prerequisite principle for our process of learning: *You cannot learn to prophesy without prophesying!* If we are truly going to learn, then we must go beyond highlighting principles and memorizing Bible verses; we must put into practice what we learn.

Now that I am able to look back on my journey and consider what I have learned, it seems right and good to lay out the principles that I feel are most important. Whether you are well-trained in the prophetic ministry or not, I believe that these principles will help you grow and become more fruitful as you deliver prophetic words to people.

Receiving a Prophetic Word

In the previous chapter, I discussed seven different ways that we receive prophetic words from the Holy Spirit (Bible, impressions, thoughts, visions, dreams, voice of God, prophetic flow). Now that we understand how God communicates with us, we need to discuss how we position ourselves in order to receive His communication.

1. Cultivate your relationship with God

I realize that this should go without saying, but I am still going to say it. Our relationship with God is more important than our service for God. God is never looking for a better performance from us; what He truly wants is a better relationship with us. Before I give anyone a process of receiving and sharing prophetic words, I must emphasize the importance of knowing and seeking God first in our lives (Matthew 6:33). Are you inviting the Holy Spirit to speak into your own heart? Do you spend regular time with God simply to know Him? Do you have a vision for your relationship with the Lord to grow? If we are going to be a

God is never looking for a better performance from us; what He truly wants is a better relationship with us.

prophetic voice to others, we must begin by inviting God's voice into our own lives as we follow Him wholeheartedly.

When Jesus taught His disciples about prayer, He showed them what a relationship with the Father should look like, especially in contrast to what could violate it:

> *When you pray, you are not to be like the hypocrites; for they love to stand and pray in the synagogues and on the street corners so that they may be seen by men. Truly I say to you, they have their reward in full. But you, when you pray, go into your inner room, close your door and pray to your Father who is in secret, and your Father who sees what is done in secret will reward you* (Matthew 6:5-6).

As you can see, Jesus began by telling His disciples how not to pray. He referenced how the religious leaders of His day used prayer to receive recognition from others. This kind of hypocrisy violates our relationship with God and, obviously, affects our ministry to people. I believe that this principle can be applied to our conversation about seeking God for prophetic words. I am sure that there are many who spend more time seeking God for prophetic words than they do just cultivating their relationship with Him. Pursuing such a course could easily corrupt our hearts and produce a similar hypocrisy that wants recognition from people. Jesus goes on in His conversation to discuss a kind of intimacy with the Father that nobody else is invited into. We must daily choose to cultivate our relationship with God and remember that pure ministry to others in the public place flows out of what we have with God in the secret place.

2. Ask God for a word during your personal prayer time

As we stay closely connected to God, we should regularly ask Him to speak to us for others. Jesus taught the principle of asking and receiving as it pertained to prayer and desiring for others to receive what they needed:

Ask, and it will be given to you; seek, and you will find; knock, and it will be opened to you. For everyone who asks receives, and he who seeks finds, and to him who knocks it will be opened. Or what man is there among you who, when his son asks for a loaf, will give him a stone? Or if he asks for a fish, he will not give him a snake, will he? If you then, being evil, know how to give good gifts to your children, how much more will your Father who is in heaven give what is good to those who ask Him! (Matthew 7:7-11)

Whenever you spend time in prayer, take out a ***journal*** and write down the names of people, your church, your business, or anything or anyone else you feel led to pray for. As you pray, write down what comes to you whether you understand it or not. Sometimes you will recognize right away that God has given you a prophetic word, and other times you will have a seed of a word that is still developing. As I have journaled my prayer time over the years, I have noticed how the Lord will develop prophetic words in my heart over a period of time. While I certainly value the spontaneous words that God will give in a church service or at the grocery store, I must emphasize that, if we are going to steward the prophetic ministry, we must go beyond the spontaneous and cultivate an ear to hear what God is saying from morning until night.

3. Ask God for a word during a church service

Regardless of whatever role we may have in our church, we should always be mindful of what God is saying to the church corporately as well as to the individuals around us. Ask God for a prophetic word on your way to a church service, and while you're attending one as well. If you feel like God has given you a corporate word that is meant for everyone, then you need to follow the protocol of the church that you attend. If God gives you a personal word for an individual around you during the church service, then try and find an appropriate moment to share it with that person. If you don't attend a church that allows for the prophetic gift, then the best thing you can do is pray for your church and meet with the leaders to discuss what you believe you are receiving from the Lord.

4. Ask God for a word throughout your day

While we are at work, the coffee shop, or even the grocery store, we must tune in to the people around us and begin to ask God for prophetic words. Ask Him things like, "What are you doing in his life?" or maybe, "What is she going through right now?" As we go about our day, we must be more concerned with ministering to people than getting from point A to point B. God is at work in people's lives all around us, and all we have to do is slow down and connect to

The primary reason that we don't receive prophetic words for people outside of the church is because we don't ask (Ja. 4:2).

what the Holy Spirit is saying to each one. The primary reason that we don't receive prophetic words for people outside of the church is because we don't ask (Ja. 4:2). Watch what God will do as you simply begin to ask Him wherever you go.

Interpreting a Prophetic Word

In my experience, the majority of mistakes people make when giving prophetic words have to do with the issue of interpretation. Obviously, there are many prophetic words that don't require an interpretation, but a good percentage of them do. The purpose of this section is to identify the additional step that we take in order to discover the meaning of a prophetic word before we share it. I can't fully explain why God gives us words that are symbolic, but I certainly appreciate the power of a picture and how it can touch our emotions. A prophetic picture has the unique ability to give several messages at the same time and speak deeply to things where mere words will always fall short.

Have you experienced this before? Have you received a picture that spoke to you deeply where words would not suffice? I sure have!

I remember participating in a prophetic seminar where I learned the importance of interpretation. The facilitators of the seminar had 20 of us line up facing west with our eyes closed. Then, an unknown person came and stood behind us as we asked God for a prophetic word to share with them. As I prayed, I saw a vision of a baseball field and, specifically, a batter who kept stepping out of the batter's box because of fear. I opened my eyes and turned around to find an older woman standing in front of me. I was caught off guard because I couldn't fathom sharing this kind of vision with this type of person. Without thinking about it, I said to her, "If you stay up at the plate, you will hit a homerun." After making this statement, I explained the details of the vision that I saw right before the instructor had us all go back to our seats. After the session, I headed out to get some coffee, and the same woman approached me and told me the vision that I shared was very profound for her. Apparently, she was the leader of an evangelism program in her church, and the entire theme and curriculum of the program was connected to baseball. To be honest, I had a hard time believing this, for multiple reasons, but this woman was not joking at all. She thanked me and assured me that she was incredibly encouraged by what I shared.

This was one of my first practical lessons about visions and interpretation. I learned how easy it can be to get it wrong and how patient we need to be to get it right. Since then I have discovered a number of principles that have helped me to minister prophetically when the metaphoric language of God is present.

1. Ask God if the vision needs interpretation

Some visions do not require an interpretation because the message is embedded in the picture itself. In my case, the baseball field was enough to speak to this woman, and I may have spoken presumptively by giving her a prophetic word at all. When she gave me feedback, it had nothing to do with the word I attached to the vision, but rather how encouraged she was regarding the vision itself. Looking back on that situation, I should have just told her the vision and asked if it meant anything to her. As I minister prophetically these days, I have learned to first ask the Lord if a vision even needs an interpretation, because sometimes it doesn't.

2. Ask God for the interpretation of the vision

When you see a vision, take a step back and ask the Lord, "What does this mean?" As you do that, wait on the Lord for a moment. If someone is in front of you while you are doing this, invite them into a prayerful waiting process by saying, "Let's go ahead and wait on the Lord for a moment and see what He has to say." Too often people are rushed through the prophetic process and end up saying something they don't mean or that doesn't quite represent the vision that God gave. One picture can mean two totally different things, so we want to develop a habit of asking for the meaning from the same one who gave us the revelation: the Holy Spirit!

3. Consider the meaning of any Bible metaphors

The Holy Spirit will often give us a vision of something that is already defined in the Bible. Ask yourself, "Is this picture in Scripture?" If the picture is in the Bible, your next question is, "What does it mean in the Bible?" For example, here are some Scriptural metaphors that God may show you as you minister prophetically:

- *HOUSE*–This can represent a nation, church, family, or your own life.
- *ROCK*–This can represent God the Father, Jesus, Abraham, or a form of judgment.
- *WATER*–This can represent the Holy Spirit, the Bible, or the ministry of the Holy Spirit.
- *LION*–This can represent the Devil, Jesus, or strength.

One time, I was praying for a woman and received a vision where she was walking up to a house with a visible hesitant reaction. She continued to inch her way into the gated yard and up to the porch, where she then stood in the threshold of the front door. All of a sudden, she jumped up out of the doorway and ran out of the front yard and down the street. I stepped back and asked the Lord what it meant. A moment later, the thoughts began to flow into my mind that this was a recent experience with a new church and had happened because of a past wound that God wanted to heal. In this instance, the house represented a church, and her reluctance and running dealt with her fear and reaction as she sought to move forward but was hindered in doing so. I ministered this word in a series of questions that enabled her to talk through each scenario. We ended up praying together that God would heal her heart and bring about restoration in community.

As we previously discussed, the house in my vision could have represented a number of things, even from a Biblical standpoint. This is why we need to constantly ask the Lord what things mean and wait on His answer before we prophesy.

4. Consider the simplest meaning of what you see

Every so often, I run into somebody who takes a prophetic metaphor and makes it more confusing that it should be. God knows just how simple we really are, and He doesn't expect us to put together some elaborate spiritual puzzle. If you are waiting on the Lord for the interpretation and don't hear Him say anything, then the vision probably has the simplest meaning possible. God is not the author of confusion; He wants to bring clarity to and through us as we prophesy.

God is not the author of confusion; He wants to bring clarity to and through us as we prophesy.

5. Ask God for clarity when you don't understand

I will be honest, there are times where I receive a vision and ask God for the interpretation without receiving any clue as to what it means. The more you prophesy, the more opportunities you will have to get stumped from time to time. Unfortunately, prophetic people generally don't tend to admit when they don't know something, so you would probably never know there was a struggle with this unless you experienced it yourself. I want to encourage you to ask God for clarity and be patient as you prophesy over people. When we prophesy, we are not in a hurry to get to the finish line. We are only responsible to hear from the Lord and prophesy what He gives us; no more and no less. Clarity is one of the greatest gifts you can give someone, so don't shortcut the process when you prophesy.

Delivering a Corporate Prophetic Word

Now that we have received a prophetic word and properly interpreted any necessary elements, what do we do now? I am sure the easy answer would be, just share it! Well, it's not quite that simple. What we do with a prophetic word depends on where we are going to share it and to whom it may concern. A corporate prophetic word is a prophecy that is meant for a group of people rather than a single individual. The group setting necessitates an understanding of a clear protocol that will allow for the word to be shared effectively with accountability.

When the apostle Paul wrote to the Corinthian church, he actually addressed the use of the prophetic gift in a corporate gathering (1 Co. 14:26-33). The church at Corinth had made a mess of spiritual gifts, which only led to confusion. Paul laid out some clear principles for the church that would serve as guidelines until maturity could be established. In my home church, we have a similar protocol for how prophetic words are given, which is primarily what I will share with you in this section.

1. *Become familiar with the church protocol*

If we have a word for our church, we must make sure to ask a leader about the protocol for prophetic sharing before we try to share it. Pastors are approached by so many people for all kinds of reasons, and our goal is not a compulsive sharing but rather a trusted relationship. Seek to understand, support, and submit to the prophetic protocol that the leadership has developed for the corporate gathering. It may not be something you agree with per se, but it must be something that you respect for the sake of unity overall.

In our church, we only allow those who are on the leadership or the prophetic team to give corporate words. The reason for this is simple: they are trusted, and well-acquainted with who we are, what we do, and how we do it. If a team member has a prophetic word for the church, they come to me during the service and tell me the word. At that point, I discern whether or not the word is for the church and whether it should be shared in cooperation with everything else that is going on. The majority of the time, we make sure that the word is shared because we want a prophetic release in our community. However, sometimes we have too much going on in the service, so we share it the following week or make room by cutting out something else.

If your church doesn't have a protocol for prophetic sharing, then make an appointment with the pastor and discuss the importance of this issue. You may be the person to help develop an important element for your church as you humbly work together with your leadership.

2. *Share positive words with a positive attitude*

I realize how this may sound, but, truthfully, prophetic people must be for the church and for the leadership of the church. The body of Christ works together as a team. There are not two competing agendas during a church service, and we need to be mindful of the condition of our hearts as we share. I am not saying that every prophetic word will be happy-clappy, health and wealth. However, the typical word spoken to a corporate gathering will be edifying, encouraging, and comforting (1 Corinthians 14:3). I can't tell you how many times I have listened to someone give a prophetic word that was unnecessarily harsh. The insecure prophetic person walks away thinking, "If people were connected to God, they would have received that word!" No, the fact is, they had a hard time with the message because the messenger sounded angry or condescending. I always coach people to think about sharing prophetic words like a good parent speaking to their children; after all, that is how God is with us.

3. Share words of correction, direction or warning with the leadership

I believe that God gives these kinds of words. I also believe that God will give these kinds of words to people who are not part of the leadership. However, these words must be shared in advance with the leadership for discernment and prayer. If the leaders decide that what has been shared with them is prophetic for the whole church, then they should share it with wisdom at the right time. I have witnessed people prophesy to the whole church with no regard to the prayerful vision of the leadership—which is ignorant at best and arrogant at worst. I encourage anyone with such a word to write it down and email it to the leaders with a humble response. Your responsibility is to bring the words that God gives you to the leaders; their responsibility is to determine what is for the church and how it should be implemented.

4. Share the prophetic word clearly and concisely

When we give a corporate prophetic word, we want to make sure that it makes sense to us before sharing it with others. I teach people when they start out to write down the word and read to the church what they wrote. This may seem like a bit of a formula, but it definitely helps prophetic people develop a clarity and brevity in their ministry that will be appreciated by those they minister to.

For some odd reason, people tend to change their tone and terminology when they give a corporate prophetic word. Here is my best advice: don't do that. There is no need to change your vocabulary or raise your voice; just speak as you normally do. Our words should embrace the culture of those we are reaching, avoiding potentially offensive slang, Christianese terminology, and KJV English (thee's and thou's).

Also, I think it's important to simply give the word without commentary or any additional thoughts. If you have a leadership role, then facilitating a response to the word may be appropriate; otherwise, it's best to leave it up to those leading the service. Church services have time constraints, and the other pastors have spent hours preparing sermons and worship sets, so we need to be mindful of this as we share. We should give our words without elaboration or exaggeration. We must seek to be as clear and concise as possible and try not to repeat ourselves, which simply trusts that people understood what we said.

5. Ask for feedback

I can honestly say that I didn't start out asking for feedback, but I wish I had, because I really see the wisdom in it now. Let me put it to you like this: feedback is your friend. If the leadership or the church felt certain things about your prophetic ministry, wouldn't you want to know it? One of the best things anyone did for me was pull me aside and say, "Hey Ben, I don't mean to offend you, but you don't need to repeat yourself when you prophesy." When I heard that, I literally thought to myself, "I don't repeat myself." How wrong I was! After that point, I really pressed into feedback regarding my prophetic words, and other ministry as well. For some reason, there is this unspoken rule that we are not supposed to give feedback about the prophetic words that are spoken. That is nonsense. Asking for and sharing feedback is how we weigh the words that are spoken, which is a biblical paradigm and should be practiced in every area of prophetic ministry (1 Th. 5:19-21; 1 Co. 14:29-33).

Delivering a Personal Prophetic Word

When you have a prophetic word for an individual, there are some different principles that apply in contrast to a corporate word. Additionally, there is a difference between prophesying over an individual in the church and someone in our everyday life. I learned the following through my own development, as well as helping many others to prophesy effectively. The order of each principle is not important but the content certainly is.

1. Pray the prophetic word

Not everyone fully understands the prophetic, so it can be helpful if you engage people in prayer before prophesying. I will typically ask someone, "Would you mind if I prayed for you?" Usually, the response is, "Sure, that's fine." At that point, I pray the prophetic word over the person, along with any other prayers that come to mind. When I finish praying, I usually take an opportunity to reiterate the prophetic word that I prayed and let them know that I really sensed God was at work in that particular way. Additionally, when you don't have a prophetic word or a full understanding of the word you have, it's best to pray over someone as a way of fully receiving from God before you prophesy to them.

2. Prophesy with clarity

The apostle Paul encouraged the Corinthian church to seek an interpretation alongside speaking in tongues (1 Co. 14:8). His premise for doing this was to help the church consider what the listeners were receiving as they exercised their gifts. I think the same principle can apply for our prophetic words. We must consider what people are hearing when we prophesy. Do they understand us? Is what I am saying confusing or clear? Do I understand what I am saying? The fact is, the clearer we are with our prophetic words, the easier it is for a person to receive them.

3. Prophesy with love

When you prophesy, it's important to speak to people in an honoring way. Remember that Jesus taught us to treat people the way we want to be treated (Lk. 6:31) This should apply also to the prophetic; prophesy to people the way you want to be prophesied to. Ask for their name, look them in the eye, and make sure that you speak to them and not at them. If you have any difficult words, handle them with the greatest of care, knowing that God deeply loves them as He does you.

4. Prophesy with Scripture

When you prophesy, consider passages of Scripture that may correlate with your prophecy and share those whenever possible. I use the prophetic ministry to draw people back to God's Word because it is our ultimate authority as we follow Jesus. In fact, all prophetic words have at least a principle connection to the Bible, so the more we use it, the better.

5. Prophesy with humility

The way we engage people with a prophetic word matters. An experienced prophet may be able to speak more directly and authoritatively, but if that's not who you are, then seek to present yourself with humility. For example, if you have a sense about someone's brother but you don't know if they have a brother, you should ask them, "Do you have a brother?" instead of saying, "I see God moving specifically in your brother's life!" I am not suggesting that this approach is prideful, but it doesn't set you up well if you are wrong. If you ask about their brother and they say they don't have a brother, you can easily redirect the conversation somewhere else instead of trying to back out of a more difficult situation.

When I prophesy, I love to ask questions as a part of my ministry. I ask questions like; "Did you ever live in another country?" or "Does the name Heather mean anything to you?" and maybe even, "Have you been praying about a specific field of education?" Asking questions as you prophesy can make a world of difference, and it really is a way of presenting yourself in a humble manner, which is easier for people to engage.

6. Prophesy with normal language

We have to remember that we function like translators. God will download a prophetic word into our heart and work with us to translate that word into a clear and understandable prophecy. Even if you are talking to a Christian, you never know if they truly understand church culture language. Just think for a moment about all the churchy words that we use on a regular basis; words like pruning, sanctification, season, breakthrough, favor, anointing, saved, etc. I really believe that we need to take big steps in the area of language if we are to be more effective in the world we live in. Most of the words we use are descriptions, not definitions, which means they are not holy in and of themselves. Find a way to say something in normal language so a person can really understand and embrace what you are saying.

7. Prophesy with accuracy

It is so important that we stay true to the word that we have received. Do not manufacture anything to produce some kind of effect or to make it greater than it really is. At the same time, you don't need to belittle the word that you have by saying, "I know you already know this," or "I know this is simple," etc. God is the giver of the revelation; we are just the messengers. If you receive an impression, say, "I received an impression." If you received a vision, say, "I received a picture." All we have to do is simply convey what we hear God say!

8. Prophesy with faith

One time, I gave a prophetic word to someone in front of a very large crowd, and the person receiving the word said, right in front of everyone, that it was not accurate. That person was with a friend who found me after the meeting and told me that the prophetic word was spot on. While I was glad to know that the word was accurate I was still discouraged that hundreds of people thought I blew it. The next time I prophesied in front of a large crowd, it required even more faith than before, and God graciously gave it to me. I wish I could say that this story was the only time that something like this happened, but that is not the case. The truth is, I have prophesied to at least a dozen people who literally told me that the word I shared was not accurate, only to find out later that it was. Also, I have made some mistakes along the way as well, which can be very discouraging.

Learning to prophesy requires a considerable amount of faith. Whether you are new at this or have been prophesying for a long time, we must continue to grow in faith for what God is going to do. Be courageous and ask God for faith as you step out because *the potential of a prophetic word is more important than the possibility of an embarrassing moment.*

Be courageous and ask God for faith as you step out because the potential of a prophetic word is more important than the possibility of an embarrassing moment.

9. Prophesy with accountability

When you prophesy, make sure that you leave room for the word to be prayed over by the person. If you say, "God told me to tell you," there is really nothing left to say. Doing this puts the other person in the very difficult position of feeling there is no freedom to ask questions or give feedback. I encourage people to stay away from using definitive language because the Bible teaches that every word should be weighed prayerfully (1 Th. 5:19-21; 1 Co. 14:29-33).

Chapter 11

Growing in the Prophetic

When our children were young, we took them to their pediatrician every few months for regular checkups. The doctor had a specific metric for evaluating the kids' development, a percentile system that measured the growth of each of the children at their relative stages in comparison to other kids. A typical report went something like this: "Your daughter is in the 20th percentile for weight and the 30th percentile for height." For a long time our kids were in the lower percentiles in both categories, which worried us at first, as young parents. As time went on, however, we became less and less concerned because, slowly but surely, the kids began to grow.

Why was I worried? Well, I was worried because it's a common and normal expectation for children to grow physically. According to the comparative metric system, my kids weren't growing at the rate of other children, and that made me nervous. We all expect physical growth because our bodies are designed for it. For a child not to grow would be abnormal, and all of us would wonder what was wrong. Do we think the same way when it comes to our spiritual growth? I certainly think we should!

When we become Christians, the Bible says that we are born again (Jn. 3:3). This is more than just a good analogy. When we give our lives to Jesus, we are immersed into a whole new life with a new heart, a new mind, and a new nature (2 Co. 5:17). Although God has given us everything we need for life and godliness (2 Pe. 1:3), we still have to grow into spiritual maturity. We are growing in knowledge, grace, discernment, wisdom, love, and faith (2 Pe. 3:18; 1 Pe. 2:2; Eph. 4:15; 2 Co. 10:15). Additionally, the call of a disciple is to make disciples, which essentially means that we help one another grow in Christ (Mt. 28:18-20).

Our need for growth is a daily spiritual reality, and it includes the area of spiritual gifts. When the apostle Paul addressed the Corinthian church regarding their misuse of prophecy, he was essentially telling them that they needed to grow in their knowledge of how to handle prophecy (1 Co. 14). When I first started out prophesying, I made many mistakes, from misinterpreting revelation to sharing words at the wrong time and in the wrong way. I wanted to grow prophetically, but I didn't know how to go about it…and no one laid out the path for me, either.

Discipleship includes the arena of the prophetic, which is why the Bible speaks about it and why you are reading this book. However, if we are really going to grow prophetically, it would be good to have some kind of roadmap to help us navigate toward maturity. In addition to what I have already shared in previous chapters, the following principles should help any person who seeks to grow beyond their current level.

Growing through Hunger

When we are physically hungry, our body tells our brain that we need to eat. Hunger pangs on a regular basis are normal because our body doesn't just want food—it needs it. Physical hunger is the strongest of human desires, which explains why the Bible uses it many times as a metaphor or parallel for spiritual desire.

The apostle Paul urged the Corinthian church to "eagerly desire" to prophesy (1 Co. 14:1). Do you desire to prophesy? Do you eagerly desire to prophesy? Do you have a spiritual hunger to receive words from God and share them with people? If we are going to grow prophetically, we need this kind of hunger to compel us to go after it.

One of the ways to cultivate a hunger to prophesy is to ask the Holy Spirit for it. This hunger that I am talking about is not man-made or something that we can produce in and of ourselves. We need the Holy Spirit to impart this desire to us, and let me assure you that He absolutely will. All you have to do is ask Him! Not only do I ask the Holy Spirit for the desire, but I ask Him for a higher level of the prophetic gift as well. We do not seek this in order to be known by people, to feel spiritual about ourselves, or to gain some kind of power, but rather to be fueled

When you know the potential that a prophetic word can bring into someone's life, it is a loving response on your part to eagerly desire that God release it through you.

by the love of God to facilitate an encounter with God. When you know the potential that a prophetic word can bring into someone's life, it is a loving response on your part to eagerly desire that God release it through you.

Another way to cultivate a hunger to prophesy is to get around people who prophesy. When I watch people minister in this way and see the powerful effect that it has in someone's life, it makes me desire it all the more. I have several prophetic friends, and the more I hang out with them and see the fruit of their ministry, the more I want to seek God to use me in the same way. We truly sharpen each other and encourage one another to not neglect the gift we have been given (1 Ti. 4:14). Our hunger for God to use us is absolutely connected to our growth because it sustains the drive that is necessary to keep going, which causes us to keep growing.

151

Growing through Purity

The prophetic gift may be a function, but it is connected to a relationship. It is possible to seek the gift in a way that violates our relationship with the Lord, which is unacceptable. Our seeking to grow prophetically is directly connected to our heart purity. An impure heart literally will cause our prophetic words to be skewed because, instead of wanting to give a gift to someone, we will be seeking something from them.

Those who minister prophetically must cultivate a pure heart before the Lord, or most assuredly they will be swayed by the fear of man or the love of self. This kind of corruption is the root of a false prophet in the making, even if that person's ministry started out right. I have seen some of the most prophetically gifted people fall the hardest because they somehow separated their function of prophecy from a pure heart before God.

The apostle Paul told his son in the faith, Timothy, that those who desire to be used as a vessel of honor must cleanse themselves from defilement and call on God with a pure heart:

> *Now in a large house there are not only gold and silver vessels, but also vessels of wood and of earthenware, and some to honor and some to dishonor. Therefore, if anyone cleanses himself from these* things, *he will be a vessel for honor, sanctified, useful to the Master, prepared for every good work. Now flee from youthful lusts and pursue righteousness, faith, love* and *peace, with those who call on the Lord from a pure heart* (2 Timothy 2:20-22).

We need to guard our hearts with all diligence (Pr. 4:23), which means that we stand watch at the gateway of our soul. What are we watching? What are we listening to? What are we reading? What conversations are we having with people? Who are we allowing to influence us and speak into our heart? Being a prophetic voice for the Lord means that we reserve our soul as a place where God can speak to and through, so we can't allow the garbage of the world to influence us.

If you needed to get some important information to another person, who would you ask to deliver it? Wouldn't you choose the most trustworthy person you know? I sure would. If we are going to be God's prophetic mouthpiece to people for whom He gave His life, we had better be those who truly lay our hearts before Him in full abandon. The gift is connected to a relationship, which means that growing in the prophetic must run congruent with our character development and spiritual maturity!

Growing through Mentorship

When I first started out in prophetic ministry, I literally had no one in my life to help me grow prophetically. I did have people who helped disciple me in many other areas, but not this one. What I learned is that mentorship comes in many forms. I drove across the state and flew across the country to attend prophetic gatherings, seminars, and conferences. I read dozens of books, listened to hundreds of teachings, and watched many hours of classes on the prophetic ministry. I even sought to learn the perspective that is completely against what I am teaching in this book. All of these resources mentored me and really helped me grow. If you are serious about growing prophetically, then I urge you to read, listen, watch, and glean as much as you possibly can. This is a form of mentorship that is available to our generation that we must take full advantage of.

When you go to the gym, you can always spot the people who clearly don't know what they're doing. Don't get me wrong; I certainly am not a professional workout person, but I know why I am there and I know what I am doing when I am there. But the only reason that I *do* know what I am doing is because several other people taught me. What would be the purpose of working out if it wasn't effective? The drive and discipline to consistently go to the gym is important, but you still need someone to teach you reps, sets, form, and endurance. The same is true for the prophetic ministry. In my opinion, the people who excel prophetically are not the most gifted, but rather, those who are the most teachable.

In my opinion, the people who excel prophetically are not the most gifted, but rather, those who are the most teachable.

While the resources were helpful, there ultimately came a point where I needed to develop a relationship with someone who had cultivated their prophetic gift beyond what I knew. To be really honest, I was waiting for people just to show up and pursue me, but that isn't how it works. I had to take responsibility for my own discipleship by pursuing people who carried something in the Lord that I could learn from. To this day, I still regularly talk with and walk with people who are shaping and sharpening voices in my life. Some of these individuals were the very ones who opened doors for me to minister beyond my influence, which catalyzed exponential growth along the way. Do you have prophetic people in your life who are farther along than you? Have you sought to pursue anyone you can learn from personally? Let me encourage you to be an initiator as you pursue mentor relationships. Don't give up if people don't respond initially, because eventually they will.

In addition to this, I must admit that it's hard to grow when you are not connected to an environment that understands, practices, and pursues the gifts of the Spirit. The fact is that oranges don't grow in Seattle, Washington, but they do in Orlando, Florida. Some environments are just not conducive for specific kinds of fruit to grow, and the same is true for the prophetic gift. I would never tell anyone to leave their church unless it was abusive, but that doesn't mean you shouldn't have a connection to a place that is developing the prophetic. I host many gatherings at my home church that welcomes and accommodates people from other churches without any pressure to stay among us. We do this to honor the churches and leaders in our area as well as the people who need to grow prophetically but shouldn't have to change churches to do it. If your church doesn't cultivate the prophetic gift, then find a place where you can connect that will help you grow but not require you to switch teams.

Growing through Failure

One of the main questions I get regarding the prophetic is, "What if I get it wrong when I prophesy?" That's a great question. Since our goal in prophesying is to deliver a word from the Lord, accuracy is very important to all of us. In our desire for accuracy, we must factor in the process of our development or we will totally miss the reality of how we grow. Without a theology for growth we will end up with a paralyzing fear that will stop us even before we try.

From a Scriptural standpoint it is hard to find good examples where people missed it prophetically. We could, potentially, look at the story of Jonah, who went through the city of Nineveh, prophesying its demise within forty days (Jon. 3:1-4). After Jonah said this, the people of Nineveh repented and their city was not overthrown, which was not mentioned anywhere in Jonah's prophecy. We could also look at the time when King David told the prophet Nathan that he wanted to build a house for the Lord, and Nathan told him, "Go, do all that is in your mind, for the Lord is with you" (2 Sa. 7:3). Not long after Nathan said this, the Lord directed him to go back to David and tell him exactly the opposite. Additionally, we could examine the case of the prophet Agabus, who might have been a little off on the details when he gave a prophetic word to the apostle Paul (Acts 21:10-14). These examples all allude to a mistake of some kind, but it's hard to verify exactly what happened. What we do know is that mistakes happen today, and they also happened with people we read about in the Bible.

Many years ago, I worked in the accounting department of a fireplace manufacturing company. Accuracy was probably the most important principle in our department because we worked with all of the invoices, billing, financing, and payments. A mistake in the accounting could be devastating on so many levels. However, we made plenty of mistakes because of data entry errors, miscommunication, and technical failures. We had a saying in our department: "As long as it doesn't leave the office, it isn't a mistake." The point of the saying was not to deny mistakes but rather to acknowledge that every mistake could be fixed unless it left our office. Once a mistake left our office, it could still be fixed, but only after costing the customer or the company a considerable amount of money. We worked hard not to make mistakes, but we worked even harder to remedy any mistakes when they happened. The question is not, "How do we avoid failure?" but, "How do we navigate through failure and learn from it?"

I have already discussed some of these things in chapter 6, but let me take a moment to clarify the difference between making a mistake and intentionally misleading others through false prophecy. Let's say I went to the store and paid for my groceries with a counterfeit bill. Would it matter if I knew whether the bill was counterfeit or not? You're darn right it would! If I intentionally used the counterfeit bill, then I willingly committed a crime, and, if caught, most likely would go to jail. On the other hand, if I wasn't aware that the bill was fake and I was caught, I would only be responsible to explain where I got the fake bill. A false prophet willingly and knowingly gives false words in order to deceive people. That is not the same thing as someone giving a prophecy that wasn't accurate but who thought it was. We still need to deal with failure and work through it, but we can't treat it the same as false prophecy from a false prophet. This means that we must start this conversation by factoring in the reality that failure will happen, and we can work through it when it does.

A false prophet willingly and knowingly gives false words in order to deceive people. That is not the same thing as someone giving a prophecy that wasn't accurate but who thought it was.

One time, during one of our conferences, I was prophesying over people from the stage. To my left, I noticed a man and a woman standing close together and made the assumption that they were married. Don't ask me why I did this, but it gets worse. I began to prophesy over them as a couple, and the longer I spoke, the more smiles I saw from the people all around them. Guess what? They weren't married, they weren't even together, and one of them was in a relationship with someone else. Both of these individuals had come with the same group from a local church in our area, and this was their first visit to our church. I blew it and was completely embarrassed. I don't even know how it happened, to be quite honest with you. That moment became a big joke for the next several months, and I am sure that these individuals will not easily forget that embarrassing night.

The first thing I had to do was _own_ the fact that I had made a mistake. I apologized to both of them as well as to their pastor. Here is a simple principle: if you *make a mistake*, then you should *make an apology*. I have seen people make a mistake in their prophetic sharing, but instead of apologizing, try to "spin" the word only to cover the fact that they actually blew it. If you can't own the failure, you can't grow from the failure. Failure provides us with an opportunity to humble ourselves, press into God, and learn from our mistakes so that we are better the next time. For me, now, almost every time I go to prophesy over a man and a woman standing next to each other, I ask this question: "Are you guys together?" Guess what? I have never made that mistake again, probably avoiding a handful of additional failures from that one hard lesson. Nobody wants to fail, but the fact is, you will. You can either grow through the failures of your past, or you can stay stuck in the fantasy of perfection.

Growing through Rejection

One of the biggest factors related to growing in the prophetic is how we handle rejection. We have to make a choice before anything ever happens: will we *go* through it or *grow* through it? You can't stop the rejection that *will* come, but you can choose to respond in a way that looks like Jesus. I would love to tell you that everyone will welcome and accept your prophetic gift, but the truth is that there will be times where you feel more tolerated than celebrated.

Jesus taught His disciples to prepare their hearts for being misunderstood, maligned, persecuted, and rejected. He used the prophets of old as an example of those who endured such treatment because of their ministry:

> *Blessed are you when* people *insult you and persecute you, and falsely say all kinds of evil against you because of Me. Rejoice and be glad, for your reward in heaven is great; for in the same way they persecuted the prophets who were before you* (Matthew 5:11-12).

How do you rejoice when you're rejected? Jesus, in this passage, helps us understand how that is even possible, and it is all about having the right perspective. First, we are not alone. Prophets, apostles, and disciples of all kinds have been rejected by their own family, churches, and surrounding communities. Second, if our ministry is pure, then our reward in heaven is great. Do we have an eternal perspective? Are we truly doing this for the Lord, or do we want the praise of men? If you seek the approval of people, you will not be able to endure in the prophetic ministry, or any ministry, for that matter (Gal. 1:10).

If you seek the approval of people, you will not be able to endure in the prophetic ministry, or any ministry, for that matter (Gal. 1:10).

Rejection is par for the course, but we must make sure that any rejection we receive is not because of our own doing. I have seen far too many with a martyr complex who literally brought criticism and controversy upon themselves. If you say or do something you shouldn't, you need to own it, humble yourself, and make it right.

You can't be harsh, weird, inaccurate, or demanding and expect total acceptance in the body of Christ. Humility goes a long way, and we must make sure that any suffering we endure is righteous and not self-inflicted (1 Pe. 3:13-17).

Rejection comes against the prophetic gift for many reasons, but you can't allow yourself to take it personally. Even as I say this, I still need to hear it. So, why do people reject the prophetic calling and gifting among us? Well, here is a short list, for starters:

• The prophetic can often shed light on sin or darkness.
• The prophetic can say what people don't want to hear.
• The prophetic can be unpredictable and therefore uncontrollable.
• The prophetic exposes the work of the demonic, to which they respond with lies and accusation.
• The prophetic reminds people that we are following Jesus and could potentially bring guilt to those who don't pray or wait for the counsel of the Lord in their life.
• The prophetic can threaten the status quo or religious traditions.

There is warfare attached to this ministry, and you need to be prepared for it. At the same time, we must fully understand that our battle is not against flesh and blood, so we are not allowed to demonize people when they reject us (Eph. 6:12). If you are being rejected, then pray for, bless, and express love toward those who are coming against you. Sometimes, when I prophesy, I am very aware that a handful of people listening would rather that I never say anything. It doesn't make things easy, but as I process it with the Lord, He always calls me to manifest the character of Christ, no matter what.

The apostle Paul talked about sharing in the "fellowship of His sufferings," which, in my opinion, includes rejection (Phil. 3:10). There is a powerful fellowship with Christ that we experience when we draw near to Him in the midst of our rejection. In that place, His approval and acceptance is all that matters, which is really the primary truth that keeps you moving forward as a prophetic person.

The growth that emerges on the other side of our fellowship with Jesus is priceless and cannot be replaced by anything else.

Growing through Stepping Out

As you know, I spent many years training people to hear from God and give prophetic words. However, I found that far too many of those who were trained never allowed it to leave the building, which, consequently, stunted their growth. When we start learning to prophesy, we usually do so in the context of the church building. If we are well trained, our ministry can move beyond those gatherings into our home, small groups, and trusted circles. While this is good, we cannot allow it to stop there. We should seek to integrate the prophetic gift into every area of our life, which includes the grocery store, restaurants, our workplace, and beyond.

Can you remember having a home telephone with the long cord? If you wanted to talk in your room, you had to get an even longer cord to make it happen. When technology advanced, we moved from the corded phone to the cordless phone. In fact, we had several cordless phone updates to where now you can probably talk on your home phone in a neighbor's house with a perfect connection. Our cordless home phones are great, but they are nothing like having a cell phone. Cell phones enable us to talk to people everywhere and anywhere. This progression of phone technology is a good metaphor for what we should seek in our prophetic development. The corded home phone is similar to being able to hear God and prophesy at the church building. The cordless phone is similar to being able to hear God and prophesy in our trusted circles beyond the church building. However, our goal is to "go cellular" with the prophetic gift, in that we can hear God and prophesy to anyone anywhere.

Jesus was not restricted by the walls of the synagogue in any of His ministry endeavors. The model and ministry of Jesus was that He did what He saw the Father doing and said what the Father told Him to say (Jn. 5:19). This should be our goal as we grow in the prophetic ministry. God wants to speak through us in every sphere of society, and we cannot allow mindsets that confine our prophetic activity to the safe places of our church buildings.

God wants to speak through us in every sphere of society, and we cannot allow mindsets that confine our prophetic activity to the safe places of our church buildings.

Practically speaking, let me encourage you to do a few very important things as you grow through stepping out beyond your comfort zone.

1. Prophesy everyday

One of my personal goals as I receive the admonition of the apostle Paul is to exercise my gift of prophecy every day (Ro. 12:6). It's not a quota or a scorecard but a reminder that God has given me something to give away, and I need to be intentional if that is going to become my reality. When you wake up in the morning and spend time with the Lord, ask Him for prophetic words for people in your day, and, with expectation, be on the lookout for the people that God wants you to speak to.

2. Stay available

Most people have full schedules and live constantly on the go. That is simply the reality that we all live in. However, if we are going to grow in the prophetic by stepping out in our daily lives, we have to make ourselves available to the Holy Spirit. We can do this by inviting the Holy Spirit into the normal moments of our day. When you start thinking about someone while you're driving, pray for them and ask the Holy Spirit for a prophetic word. When you are texting with a family member or friend, ask the Holy Spirit for a word to send to them. When you are at meetings and sitting next to people you don't know, ask the Holy Spirit for a word. Staying available means that we are mindful throughout our day that God wants to move in and through us beyond the minutia of our daily tasks.

3. Take risks

Stepping out in the prophetic means that we need to take some risks. I have taken many risks, and, for the most part, don't regret any of them even when I was rejected. What I do regret is not taking certain risks, because it was a lost opportunity that could have been a powerful prophetic moment. The amazing testimonies that inspire and challenge us are always on the other end of our obedience. I have prophesied over people at schools, coffee shops, airports, baseball games, and even on sidewalks while walking around my neighborhood. After experiencing so many incredible moments, I have realized that what I once thought was a risk was really an invitation to partner with the Holy Spirit. There must come a point where we realize that, in order to grow, we have to step beyond what we know.

Chapter 12

Developing a Prophetic Church

One of the great privileges of my life is the opportunity to travel quite a bit and minister alongside a number of local churches. I love visiting new churches, meeting new people, and observing the diversity throughout the body of Christ. I consider it a serious honor to get to do what I do. Churches invite me to do a number of things: preach, lead retreats, host seminars, keynote conferences, prophesy during a night of prayer. I am probably most known for my prophetic ministry, so almost every invitation I receive comes with an expectation that I will prophesy over the church or individuals.

Don't get me wrong; I love prophesying, but something I love even more is helping to develop prophetic churches that exercise the gift on a regular basis. When I was younger, I was content with doing most of the ministry myself, but over the years I have come to see the importance of equipping the entire church to walk in a greater fullness. If a church had three hundred people and I spent a few days with them, I could probably give thirty different people a prophetic word. As you can see, that's only 10% of the people, and I usually only visit once a year, if I am able. However, if I could equip thirty people to give ten prophetic words throughout the year, then

100% of the church would receive from the prophetic gift. Furthermore, what would happen if I could equip three hundred people to give ten prophetic words throughout the year? The obvious fruit of this kind of equipping is what inspires my vision to develop prophetic churches, and not just a few prophetic people.

When we equip the whole church to minister, we not only accomplish more, but we also activate everyone to be doers of the Word at the same time (Ja. 1:22-25). My heart's desire is that all God's people would hear His voice and prophesy! For this to actually happen, we must develop prophetic churches that have a vision to inspire and instruct a culture to hear and heed the voice of God together. Do we want a prophetic event, or a prophetic church? Do we want a few gifted people, or do we want to the whole church trained to hear God's voice and prophesy? If we want a prophetic church, we must take the necessary steps to move beyond where we are with courage and clarity.

When we equip the whole church to minister, we not only accomplish more, but we also activate everyone to be doers of the Word at the same time (Ja. 1:22-25).

I am not merely an advocate for the prophetic ministry; I believe wholeheartedly that every church should be developed to continue the whole ministry of Jesus. As we focus on developing a prophetic church, I think we are really saying that discipleship is about equipping the whole church to do the work of the ministry, instead of just a special few (Eph. 4:11-16). The apostle Paul told the *whole* Corinthian church to eagerly desire the prophetic because of the benefit that the *whole* church receives. (1 Co. 14:1). Developing a prophetic church means that we move the gift of prophecy from a novelty to normalcy.

So many books focus on encouraging prophetic individuals rather than developing prophetic churches. In this book I wanted to somehow do both. If you are a leader, I want to encourage you to catch a vision for developing a prophetic church. If you are not a leader, I hope that by reading this book you will catch a vision for how you could help your church build a prophetic ministry that touches and trains everyone.

Build a Prophetic Team

One of the first steps in developing a prophetic church is to build a team. I never thought about this in my earlier days, nor had I ever heard about something like it from anyone else. However, I have come to see the wisdom of putting together a team in order to create space and place for the prophetic gift to benefit the whole church.

Building a prophetic team is good for many reasons, but the primary purpose is to disciple those in the church who are prophetically gifted. Most churches have a handful of prophetic people, and our job is to help identify who they are and invite them into a community where they can grow and become a fruitful voice among us. Too many prophetic people end up doing their own thing in their own way, which often becomes disconnected from the church as a whole. My hope is that establishing prophetic teams can help prevent some of the isolation and weirdness that so easily can be attached to the prophetic ministry at large.

In our church, I invited 15 individuals to be on our prophetic team. All of our team members either have a prophetic gift or a heart for intercession. We meet every other month for community, training, prayer, and dialog as we seek the word of the Lord for our congregation. In between our gatherings we do several things as well. First, we all read a book that focuses on the prophetic ministry together for training purposes. Second, I send a few emails per month with a prophetic prayer focus regarding one of our ministries or something beyond the four walls of our church. In these emails I ask our team members to pray over something specific and send back any words that they receive from the Lord. Then, I take those words and put all of them in a document that I edit and finalize before sending it to the person who is directly involved with the specific prayer focus for that week. Can you imagine being a youth pastor and receiving a document with 5-10 prophetic words for you, your ministry, your kids, and what God wants to do? The heart of our team is to provide prophetic insight for every leader, ministry, and specific individuals in our church.

In addition to this, our prophetic team is trusted to share corporate words during our church services as well as our worship and prayer gatherings. When a team member has a word, I walk up on the stage with them, introduce them by name as part of our prophetic team, and let them prophesy. Once they are done, I remind everyone that we are a church that believes the Holy Spirit speaks to us and invites us into a response. Helping the church to understand these things is part of developing a prophetic culture that can be trusted and validated over the years of serving God together. The team approach is a powerful aid to developing a prophetic church because it not only produces prophetic words, but also provides a great example because it is made up of people from the congregation.

Empower a Prophetic Culture

Developing a prophetic church requires us to cultivate a culture that not only welcomes but practices the gift of prophecy in a very regular way. Building a prophetic team will be counterproductive in developing a prophetic church if we don't empower a culture alongside it. I have found these principles to be especially important for empowering a prophetic culture:

1. Develop prophetic vision

You cannot empower a prophetic culture without a clear vision. This means that we do the hard work of writing out WHAT we believe and WHY we believe it. This could look like a handful of statements with Scriptures attached to it that will need to be followed up with training and protocol. For example:

- We believe that every Christian can hear the voice of God (Jn. 10:27).
- We believe that every Christian can prophesy (Acts 2:17-21; 1 Co. 14:1).
- We believe that the prophetic gift strengthens the church (1 Co. 14:3).
- We believe that God will give us prophetic direction as we pray (Acts 13:1-3).

These points could all be summed up with a clear vision statement that says, "The church is a prophetic people who can hear the voice of God and prophesy through the power of the Holy Spirit." Once you have a vision statement you can begin to share it with the church on a regular basis with the goal that it will be embedded into the life flow of the church.

2. Implement prophetic training

Now that we have a vision statement, we need to implement periodic training for the whole church and not just the prophetic team. At our church we have several approaches to this. First, we occasionally have a sermon series on hearing the voice of God during our Sunday morning gatherings. Additionally, we offer two classes in this area that provide a biblical and practical foundation for every person at our church. The first class is called "Hearing God's Voice," and is focused entirely on hearing the voice of God personally. The second class, called "The Prophetic Ministry," complements the first by focusing entirely on hearing the voice of God prophetically as we learn to prophesy.

In addition to these classes, we reference and recommend some specific resources that will help to develop our language and practice as a prophetic church. As you may have guessed, we specifically use my resources at our church, but we also use a few others as well. Don't get me wrong; I am all for people reading and gleaning from as much as possible. However, I have noticed in my travels how often leadership, teams, and churches are not unified in their thoughts and practice because they each emphasize different principles from different authors. I recommend that each church choose a few specific books that, alongside Scripture, are required reading as they develop the principles and protocols that they will implement.

3. Encourage prophetic release

Once regular prophetic training has been established, we must be dedicated to encouraging the church to minister to one another prophetically. We want the prophetic gift to be so normal that someone could go to any small group, youth gathering, or Bible study and expect to give or receive a prophetic word.

One practical tip would be to encourage people at all the prayer gatherings to listen to the Lord and share whatever they receive. Sometimes, when I facilitate pre-service prayer, I take a moment to wait on the Lord and then ask if anybody received something prophetic. When someone shares a prophetic picture or word, we respond by praying that God would do the very thing that He just showed us. All of this brings a normalcy and familiarity to the voice of the Holy Spirit among the people throughout the various ministries of the church.

The church needs to be encouraged to prophesy even when they know that they can. Even the apostle Paul had to remind Timothy to put his gift into use: "For this reason I remind you to kindle afresh the gift of God which is in you through the laying on of my hands" (2 Ti. 1:6). If you're a leader and you want a prophetic church, you have to learn to give the ministry away to others instead of doing it all

If you're a leader and you want a prophetic church, you have to learn to give the ministry away to others instead of doing it all yourself.

yourself. Sure, I could prophesy during all of our gatherings, but all that would do is put a spotlight on me, frustrate the people, and hold back the full release of what God brings through His body. Instead, I must encourage the people to stir up the gifts and put them into practice, even if it means that I hold back so that others can step forward.

4. Celebrate prophetic fulfillment

Wherever you have a release of true prophecy you can expect the fulfillment of prophecy. We need to record the words that God gives to us so that we can intercede and rejoice together when they come to pass. The healthiest prophetic cultures I have ever seen do two things really well. They train the people to prophesy beyond the walls of the church building, and they share the testimonies of God's fulfillment with regularity. Celebrating what God has done is such a healthy part of the body of Christ, and certainly part of a prophetic church.

Preserve the Prophetic Ministry

There is an important undercurrent that must be a part of this entire process if we are to preserve a healthy prophetic church over the long haul. I am referring to the process of discerning and weighing prophetic words as they are shared. I can think of only a few churches that I have ever been around that implement principles of testing and weighing either corporate or personal prophetic words.

When the apostle Paul wrote to the Thessalonian church, it seems clear that, at one point, they welcomed prophets to speak to them. From the text it would seem that these supposed prophets declared that Jesus had already returned, which caused quite an uproar among the church. Therefore, Paul laid out a clear understanding of the return of Jesus so they would be at peace (1 Thess. 4:13-5:11). This unfortunate abuse of the prophetic gift caused the Thessalonians to do what many do with the prophetic gift today:

shut it down entirely. While the abuses were very real, Paul sought to deter them from this reaction by giving the following admonition:

> Do not **quench** the Spirit; do not **despise** prophetic utterances. But **examine** everything carefully; **hold fast** to that which is good (1 Thessalonians 5:19-21, emphasis added).

Paul begins by telling the church not to "quench" the Holy Spirit. By quench he means not to hinder what the Spirit wants to do, which specifically refers to people giving prophetic words. Obviously, they were not interested in hearing prophetic words because of the past abuse that they endured. These past abuses pushed the church to the point where they actually "despised" prophecy, meaning that they felt it was worthless. Paul seeks to lead them out of this mindset by encouraging them to examine all prophecies, or put every word to the test. The goal of testing a prophetic word is to truly receive from the Lord. If we automatically resist prophetic words when they are spoken, we are potentially missing what the Lord is saying and wanting to do in our lives.

While the Thessalonian church needed some help in order to receive again, the Corinthian church was in an entirely different place. The church at Corinth was a mess. They sought to exercise a kind of spirituality that was self-serving and flamboyant, to say the least. Paul gave them several admonitions in the hope that they would become spiritually sound and helpful to those who would receive from their ministry. In essence, Paul needed to help them prune their ministry so they could be fruitful again. He told them that all New Testament prophecy is a partial view (1 Co. 13:9) of what God is saying and needs to be weighed carefully by other prophetic people (1 Co. 14:29).

In essence, Paul needed to PROVOKE the Thessalonian church and PRUNE the Corinthian church, with the goal of PRESERVING the prophetic ministry among both churches. In order to preserve the prophetic ministry, we must know how to test the prophetic. I have developed a short and practical list that can help do just that.

1. Prophetic words should be recorded

With today's technology, there are all kinds of ways to record a prophetic word. I regularly have people ask me if they can record on their phone a word that I give them, and my answer is always, "Absolutely." I personally prefer to write words down whenever possible, but regardless of how it's done, we should be mindful of having an accurate record of the prophecies that we give and receive.

2. Prophetic words should be understood

If we are given a word and it doesn't make sense, there is no law against asking the person to clarify what they saw or heard so that we can better understand it. When people ask me a question about a word that I shared with them, I am always glad to clarify anything that I can. Sometimes, we are not able to get more clarity on a word, but if we really need it, I think that it's worth asking for.

3. Prophetic words should be scriptural

Not every prophetic word needs to have a Bible verse attached to it, but, at the very minimum, it must not contradict the Bible. Additionally, it is my conviction that all prophetic words find their root system in Scripture, at least principally. Therefore, we must diligently connect the dots of Scripture and prophecy as we test what is from God.

4. Prophetic words should be congruent

Sometimes a prophetic word goes against everything that you have previously heard from God yourself. Therefore, if we don't receive a new direction from the Lord personally, it's safe to assume that the word is not accurate. Prophetic words must be congruent with what God has already spoken to us and with those things that have been well established in our lives.

5. Prophetic words should be confirmed

When we receive a prophetic word about something we have not previously considered, we need to ask the Holy Spirit to confirm it. Discernment is so vital in the weighing process that we must be diligent to ask God to help us know what is from Him.

6. Prophetic words should be accountable

If the prophetic word goes beyond something simple, we should always invite trusted friends into the discernment process. We hear God the best in community, so make sure to share prophetic words with people you know who truly walk with the Lord.

7. Prophetic words should be reviewed

Not every prophetic word can be confirmed quickly, nor should it be. Therefore, it is best to lay the word aside and keep moving in what is in front of you. However, it is a good practice to periodically review the things that you have heard from others and see if you have received any further clarity or discernment. I personally have a document on my computer that has a few pages with words that I don't know what to do with. Every few months I review the document prayerfully to see if anything has changed.

These seven principles can truly help us preserve the prophetic ministry as we develop a prophetic church together. Following solid principles like these will breed a healthy culture, which is exactly what we want in our churches!

Protect the Prophetic Integrity

Whenever I talk to someone about the prophetic ministry, I can often tell if they have been affected by a version of it that was harmful or just plain weird. I totally understand that there are churches and individuals out there that give a bad name to the prophetic. I have a lot of compassion for people who have been negatively affected by the stuff that is called prophetic, but which is strange, over-spiritual, unhealthy, or worse. I also understand why so many pastors would rather not deal with any of it because of the potential problems that it can bring. With that said, I still think we can recover the true purpose and power of the prophetic ministry in our churches. But that will only happen with intentionality.

I was in a church service once when all of a sudden, during the middle of worship, some unknown lady about ten rows back started yelling out a prophetic word. I couldn't really hear what she was saying, and even if I could, it wasn't very understandable anyway. The pastor of the church tolerated the outburst for about ten seconds before he grabbed a microphone, walked up on the stage, and, lovingly, asked her to stop. We all knew that the pastor had to bring correction to her, but when he did, I felt like several people in the room thought he was wrong for doing it. That was the strange part for me. The awkwardness of the correction felt stronger than the awkwardness of the outburst.

This scenario is something that I have experienced several times as a leader. During one of our conferences, I observed a few young men make their way around the sanctuary, ministering to various young women. I had never seen any of these guys before, so I approached them and asked if we could speak in the lobby. When we got outside, I told them that I had observed them praying for people during the ministry time and asked if they knew any of the people they were praying for. One of the guys specifically said to me, "No, I just started praying for whoever the Holy Spirit told me to pray for." I then told him that we don't allow anybody we don't know personally to minister to people at our church or during our conferences. He replied, "Well, I have to obey God and not man, so I am sure you can understand." At that point I knew this wasn't going to get any better, so I just cut straight to the point and said, "Outside this church, you are free to do as you want, but while you are among us as a guest, you are not allowed to do that, or you will have to leave." This conversation continued for a few more minutes until I politely asked them all to leave.

One of the reasons we have so much prophetic weirdness is because we don't bring the necessary correction. In both of the stories I just shared, it was rather obvious that there were people present who felt like the correction was harsh, immature, and unnecessary. It's actually quite the opposite, and that's part of the problem. Leaders need to lead. Sometimes the people don't understand how the correction fits in with grace, tolerance, releasing the gifts, etc. But I can tell you that it's far better to correct a situation when it happens than to kick the can down the road and hope it gets better. It won't get better, and that is why we have churches that disallow the prophetic or capitulate to an "anything goes" model. Do you recognize the "either/or" approach from the previous churches that we studied (Thessalonian and Corinthian)?

One of the reasons we have so much prophetic weirdness is because we don't bring the necessary correction.

So many of us are tired of prophetic weirdness, so we must be diligent as we deal with it. In doing that, I may appear as someone who isn't "open," or who even "quenches" the Spirit. The truth is quite the opposite. I just happen to know what will happen if we either allow the weirdness or disallow the prophetic, and neither response is biblical or reasonable. I do have compassion for people who have been a part of prophetically weird environments, and I do want to help them integrate and became fruitful. With this in mind, I regularly have hard conversations with people who are definitely misunderstood in their prophetic sharing because we owe it to one another to be honest and seek the growth of the church, even at the cost of relationship.

Something as precious as the prophetic gift will be misused, misunderstood, and even attacked. Knowing this, we are responsible to correct anything and everything when it goes off course so we can ensure that we have the best of the best among our people. I believe that protecting prophetic integrity is important to keep us moving forward as we develop a prophetic church!

Endnotes

1 John Paul Jackson, *Unmasking the Jezebel Spirit*. (Flower Mound: Streams Creative House, 2014).

2 *New American Standard Exhaustive Concordance of the* Bible, Robert L. Thomas, ed. (Nashville: B&H Publishing Group, 1981), *nebuah*, Strong's number 5016.

3 *New American Standard Exhaustive Concordance, naba*, Strong's number 612a.

4 R. Laird Harris, Bruce K. Waltke, and Gleason L. Archer, Jr., *Theological Wordbook of the Old Testament*. (Chicago: Moody Publishers, 2003), *naba*, p. 544.

5 *New American Standard Exhaustive Concordance, prophêteia*, Strong's number 4394.

6 W. E. Vine, Merrill F. Unger, and William White, Jr., *Vine's Complete Expository Dictionary of Old and New Testament Words*. (Nashville: Thomas Nelson Publishers, 1984, 1996), Kindle edition, Location 39892.

7 Joseph H. Thayer, *Thayer's Greek-English Lexicon of the New Testament: Coded with Strong's Concordance Numbers*. (Peabody: Hendrickson Publishers, Reissue, 1995), 552.

8 *New American Standard Exhaustive Concordance, prophêteuô*, Strong's number 4395.

9 *Vine's Complete Expository Dictionary*, Kindle edition, Location 39907.

10 *New American Standard Exhaustive Concordance of the* Bible, Strong's number 5030.

11 *Theological Wordbook of the Old Testament*, 544.

12 *Theological Wordbook of the Old Testament*, 823.

13 https://www.britannica.com/topic/White-House-press-secretary

14 *Holman Illustrated Bible Dictionary*, Chad Brand, Charles Draper, Archie England, eds. (Nashville: Holman Bible Publishers, 2003), 841.

15 *The Didache: The Teaching of the Twelve Apostles*, R. Joseph Owles, trans. (Createspace Independent Pub, 2014), 20-21.

16 https://www.merriam-webster.com/dictionary/disillusioned

ABOUT THE AUTHOR

Benjamin Dixon is the Director of Ignite Global Ministries, with a vision to equip the church in order to impact the world. Ben is also the author of *Hearing God* and the founder of Immersion Discipleship School, an online discipleship program that has equipped thousands to know God personally and reach people effectively. Together with his wife Brigit, they have four kids and live in Snohomish, Washington.

facebook.com/PastorBenDixon

instagram.com/MrBenDixon

twitter.com/MrBenDixon

IGNITE
GLOBAL MINISTRIES

Ben's ministry brings practical wisdom through solid biblical teaching and clear prophetic ministry that goes beyond the four walls of the church. His ministry imparts confidence in hearing God's voice and conviction for reaching people everywhere with the gospel of Jesus Christ.

If you are interested in having Ben minister in your church or at your event, please contact him through the information below and he will prayerfully consider your request.

Ignite Global Ministries Website: www.IgniteGlobalMinistries.org
Immersion Discipleship School: www.ImmersionDiscipleshipSchool.com
Ignite Global Ministries Email: info@igniteglobalministries.org

 facebook.com/igniteglobalmin

 instagram.com/igniteglobal

 twitter.com/IgniteGlobalMin

 youtube.com/IgniteGlobalMinistries

Ignite Global Office Phone: (425) 239-6528

If you really want to hear God in your life then your focus must be to know him not just to know about him. —*Hearing God*

In Benjamin Dixon's first book, *Hearing God*, he explores what it means to hear the voice of God in our everyday lives. With Biblical clarity and practical insight, this book tackles a topic that is often misunderstood and confusing in the midst of a generation that truly wants to know if God is speaking today. This book will challenge you to study God's word, deepen your prayer life and obey the voice of the Holy Spirit.

★★★★★

"All of us can hear God's voice sometimes we just need real help to discern how to discover this real relationship with God. This book is that help."
–Phil Manginelli
Lead Pastor of The Square

★★★★★

"As a ministry handbook, *Hearing God*, is conversational, practical, and doable. You'll find yourself saying, 'It can't be that simple.' But it is!"
–Daniel A. Brown, PhD
Author of *Embracing Grace* and *The Journey*

AVAILABLE FOR PURCHASE WHEREVER BOOKS ARE SOLD.